Patchwork and Quilting
Book Number 4

Kaffe Fassett • Roberta Horton • Mary Mashuta
Liza Prior Lucy • Kim Hargreaves • Pauline Smith • Sally B Davis
Rose Verney • Brandon Mably • Eleanor Yates

A   ROWAN   PRODUCTION

First Published in Great Britain in 2002 by
Rowan Yarns
Green Lane Mill
Holmfirth
West Yorkshire
England
HD9 2DX

Art Director:	Kim Hargreaves
Technical Editors:	Ruth Eglinton and Pauline Smith
Co-ordinator:	Kathleen Hargreaves
Patchwork Designs:	Kaffe Fassett, Liza Prior Lucy, Pauline Smith, Kim Hargreaves, Roberta Horton, Mary Mashuta, Rose Verney, Sally B. Davis, Brandon Mably and Eleanor Yates
Quilters:	Judy Irish and Terry Clark
Photographer:	Mark Scott
Styling:	Gail Abbott
Design Layout:	Les Dunford
Illustrations:	Ruth Eglinton and Jon Dunford
Feature:	Kathryn Samuel
Cover Photography:	Polly Wreford
Cover Styling:	Mary Norden
Cover Design:	Georgina Rhodes
Machine thread:	Drima and Sylko in UK, Coats Dual Duty Polyester USA

British Library Cataloguing in Publication Data
Rowan Yarns
Patchwork and Quilting
ISBN 0-9540949-6-4

Colour reproduction by Chroma Graphics (Overseas) Pte. Ltd
Printed and bound in Singapore by KHL Printing Co. Pte. Ltd.

CONTENTS

INTRODUCTION

Welcome to Patchwork and Quilting Book Number 4.

Its incredible how time flies and we are now introducing you to the fourth book in the Rowan series. With each new book we endeavour to challenge and inspire you with design, colour and pattern.

We have designs by Kaffe Fassett, Liza Prior Lucy, Pauline Smith, Kim Hargreaves, Brandon Mably, Sally B. Davis, Rose Verney and Eleanor Yates. We are pleased that once again Roberta Horton has designed a quilt and, for this book, has been joined by her sister, Mary Mashuta, whose reputation is also firmly established on both sides of the Atlantic.

The fabric range has once again been increased. The shot cottons now total forty three with the introduction of seven new shades, among them Lime, Jade and Cobalt. These team-up brilliantly with the four new prints Kaffe has designed:. Floral Dance, Chrysanthemum, Dotty and Bubbles. With all the colourways, a total of twenty two new prints are available in this mouthwatering selection. We hope you will have fun using them.

It was fascinating to unfold each project as it arrived at Rowan, discover which fabrics the designer had chosen and how they had been placed in the design. This year we have more appliqué and curved shapes, different techniques have been used and to help, we have expanded the appliqué section in the Patchwork Know-how (page 101) Hand or Machine? The choice is yours! For those of you who prefer to stitch by hand, Brandon's 'Raindrops' Quilt is an excellent project to embark on.

To help you with fabric selection we have given both the name and code of each fabric used in the materials section at the beginning of each project. You will also find flat photographs to complement the more artistic shots.

"WE LOVE LUCY" see page 30. The way in which Liza energises all those around her and in particular how she works with Kaffe Fassett is brought to life in this absorbing profile, written by Kathryn Samuel.

We hope you enjoy the book and look forward to seeing the results at forthcoming quilt shows.

Happy Quilting!

Ruth Eglinton and Pauline Smith

Umbrella by
Kaffe Fassett

*Opposite Boxcars by
Kaffe Fassett, this page
Plaids Squared
by Sally B Davis*

7

This page
Birds In The Air
by Roberta Horton,
opposite page Salsa
by Kim Hargreaves

This page Hazy Sunshine
by Mary Mashuta,
opposite Little Bottles
by Kaffe Fasssett

10

*Opposite Nursery Teatime by
Rose Verney, this page Bobbins
by Pauline Smith, Bars, Diamonds
In A Square and Amish Baskets
cushions all by Liza Prior Lucy*

13

*Opposite Smoky Stars
by Liza Prior Lucy,
this page Birdboxes
by Kaffe Fassett*

15

This page Attic Windows
by Kaffe Fassett,
opposite Melon Balls
by Liza Prior Lucy

16

Opposite Casbah, this page
Beasties and Twiggy cushions
all by Pauline Smith

*This page Bobbins by
Pauline Smith, opposite
Chrysanthemum Soft
Squares by Kaffe Fassett*

*Raindrops by
Brandon Mably,
opposite Marquetry
Strip Baby Quilt by
Kaffe Fassett*

22

Hundreds & Thousands
by Eleanor Yates

THE KAFFE FASSETT FABRIC COLLECTION

100% Cotton

Fabric width 45ins (114cm)

Shot Cotton

SC 01 Ginger | SC 02 Cassis | SC 03 Prune | SC 04 Slate | SC 05 Opal | SC 06 Thunder

SC 07 Persimmon | SC 08 Raspberry | SC 09 Pomegranate | SC 10 Bittersweet | SC 11 Tangerine | SC 12 Chartreuse

SC 13 Navy | SC 14 Lavender | SC 15 Denim Blue | SC 16 Mustard | SC 17 Sage | SC 18 Tobacco

SC 19 Lichen | SC 20 Smoky | SC 21 Pine | SC 22 Pewter | SC 23 Stone Grey | SC 24 Ecru

SC 25 Charcoal

The story behind Kaffe's Patchwork fabric range is an interesting one. Each year he gives some time to assist artisans around the world, and the stripes, checks and plains in this range are all individully woven on simple hand looms, through the Fair Trading Trusts in India. Being hand-woven, this means that no two fabrics are identical, and the small imperfections that occur in the process all add to the inherent beauty of these cloths. This makes for some very exciting design possibilities, whether you're following our suggested colour recipes, or working out your own.

THE KAFFE FASSETT FABRIC COLLECTION

100% Cotton

Fabric width 45ins (114cm)

Shot Cotton

SC 26 Duck Egg   SC 27 Grass   SC 28 Blush   SCV 29 Putty   SC 30 Custard   SC 31 Mushroom

SC 32 Rosy   SC 33 Water Melon   SC 34 Lemon   SC 35 Sunshine   SC 36 Lilac   SC 37 Coffee

SC 38 Biscuit   SC 39 Apple   SC 40 Cobalt   SC 41 Jade   SC 42 Rush   SC 43 Lime

Roman Glass

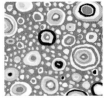 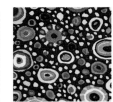 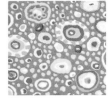 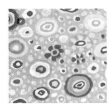 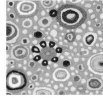 

GP 01-L   GP 01-J   GP 01-S   GP 01-C   GP 01-P   GP 01-G

Artichokes

 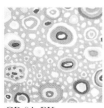 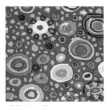   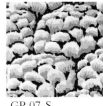

GP 01-BW   GP 01-PK   GP 01-R   GP 07-L   GP 07-J   GP 07-S

Forget-me-not Rose

  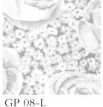 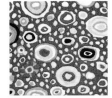  

GP 07-C   GP 07-P   GP 08-L   GP 08-J   GP 08-S   GP 08-C

THE KAFFE FASSETT FABRIC COLLECTION

100% Cotton

Fabric width 45ins (114cm)

Dotty

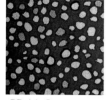 GP 14-C

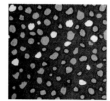 GP 14-P

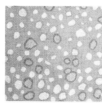 GP 14-O

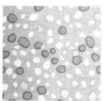 GP 14-T

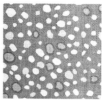 GP 14-D

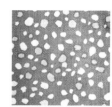 GP 14-L

Bubbles

 GP 14-SG

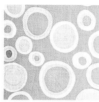 GP 15-O

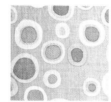 GP 15-G

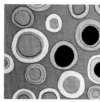 GP 15-P

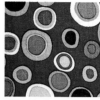 GP 15-C

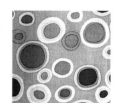 GP 15-S

Pressed Roses

 PR 01

 PR 02

 PR 03

 PR 04

 PR 05

 PR 06

Floral Dance

 PR 07

 GP 12-MG

 GP 12-O

 GP 12-MV

 GP 12-B

 GP 12-P

Damask

 GP 02-L

 GP 02-J

 GP 02-S

 GP 02-C

 GP 02-P

GP 02-CT

Flower Lattice

  GP 11-L

 GP11-J

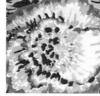 GP 11-S

 GP 11-C

 GP 11-P

 GP11-SU

The Kaffe Fassett Fabric Collection

100% Cotton

Fabric width 45ins (114cm)

Rowan Stripe

    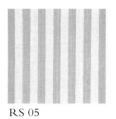 

RS 01   RS 02   RS 03   RS 04   RS 05   RS 06

Ombre Stripe

  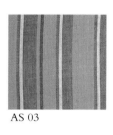 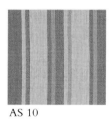 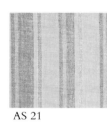 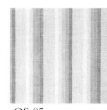

RS 07   RS 08   OS 01   OS 02   OS 04   OS 05

Blue and White Stripe   Alternate Stripe

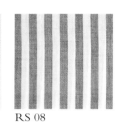    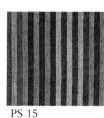 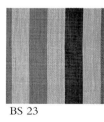

BWS 01   BWS 02   AS 01   AS 03   AS 10   AS 21

Pachrangi Stripe

 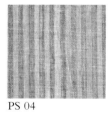 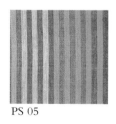 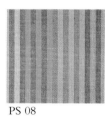 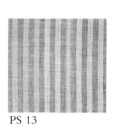 

PS 01   PS 04   PS 05   PS 08   PS 13   PS 15

Broad Stripe

  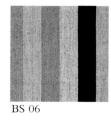  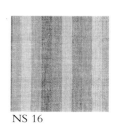 

PS 22   BS 01   BS 06   BS 08   BS 11   BS 23

Narrow Stripe

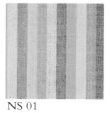 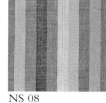 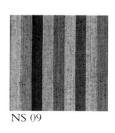  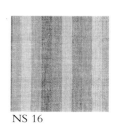 

NS 01   NS 08   NS 09   NS 13   NS 16   NS 17

THE KAFFE FASSETT FABRIC COLLECTION

100% Cotton

Fabric width 45ins (114cm)

Narrow Check

Broad Check

NC 01

NC 02

NC 03

NC 05

BC 01

BC 02

Exotic Check

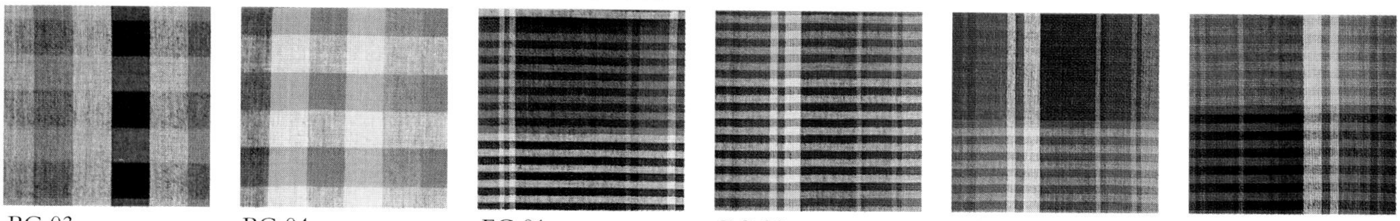

BC 03

BC 04

EC 01

EC 02

EC 03

EC 05

Exotic Stripe

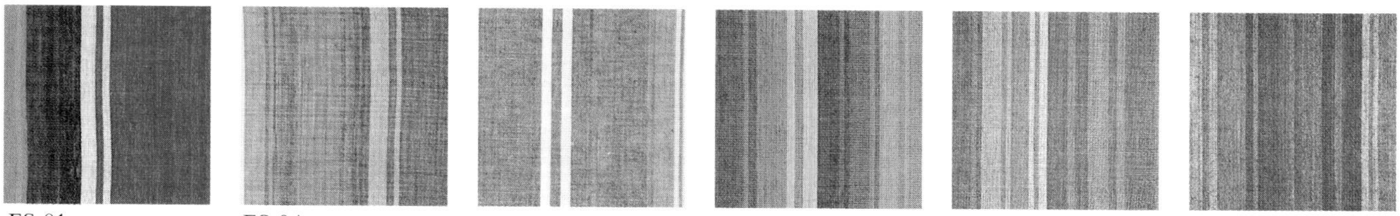

ES 01

ES 04

ES 06

ES 10

ES 15

ES 16

Gazania

ES 20

ES 21

ES 23

GP 03-L

GP 03-J

GP 03-S

Chard

GP 03-C

GP 03-P

GP 09-L

GP 09-J

GP 09-S

GP 09-C

Chrysanthemum

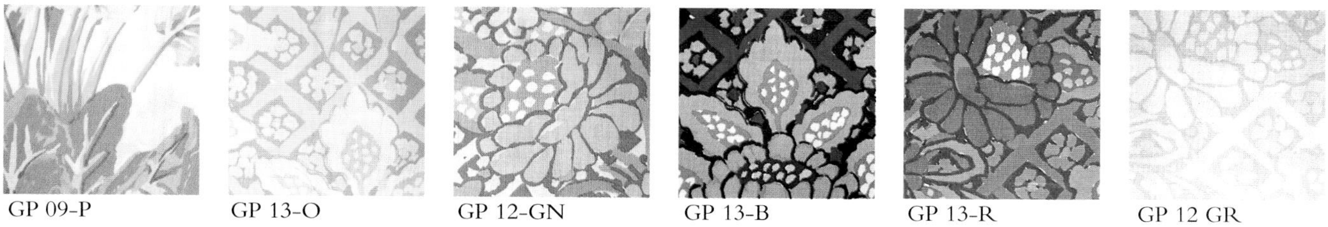

GP 09-P

GP 13-O

GP 12-GN

GP 13-B

GP 13-R

GP 12 GR

WE LOVE LUCY

If it was not for American designer Liza Prior Lucy it is possible that Kaffe Fassett might never have embraced patchwork. And without her infectious enthusiasm for spreading the word on patchwork, quilting and colour it is very unlikely that this magazine – now in it's fourth issue – would have been born. She is a wonderfully warm character who seems to energise everyone she meets. The Rowan team obviously hold her in the greatest affection. Tragedy and chance have played a crucial role in her life; she has overcome the former and grabbed the latter with gusto. By Kathryn Samuel

This page: Liza pictured with daughters Elizabeth and Alexandra and English Bulldog Delilah,
opposite page, views of the family home and cottage garden.

very Wednesday afternoon in New Hope, Pennsylvania, USA, ten women meet to quilt and sew their patchwork, rotating through each other's houses. They are a disparate group in many ways. One is a psychiatrist, another a cleaning lady, several are housewives, another is a teacher and one is Liza Prior Lucy. " It's a kind of group therapy." She told me. "All our circumstances are very different. We discuss our joys, hopes, the dodgy mammogram, our children - and we eat. Eating is a big part of it - the person who is the hostess makes a dessert - we're very inventive with baking." This is the nostalgic picture we all have of the American patchwork tradition and it is impossibly romantic to think it still exists. Liza Prior Lucy's roots may be there but she has never been able to sit still for long.

Fresh out of college and recently married, she opened a needlepoint and knitting boutique in Washington DC in 1976. Her training in clinical psychology (while devising knitting patterns for Vogue as a sideline) had taught her about the enjoyment and sense of achievement craftwork could bring. The shop was a huge success on many levels. Nancy Reagan commissioned a needlepoint chair as the official US gift to Prince William on his birth. Actresses, like Jane Seymour, were fans, using needlepoint as a way to while away back-stage waiting time. Most satisfying to Liza were the journalists like Sally Quinn and Jacqueline Adams who filled in the long gaps between news action by sewing. " It was the height of the women's lib movement. When they both won needlework prizes in some competition and I think they were more tickled and proud of that achievement than any media award "

Then very suddenly, Liza's husband died. She was just 29 years old. Pesticides had been a crucial factor in his illness and she began a strong campaign, continued today, against their use. "The shop and customer's demands became a little hard to appreciate then. I just wanted to start life over again - so I closed the shop down and moved to Pennsylvania and became a sales rep for yarn companies selling knitting wool to stores across The States." Although she is typically positive about the change of roles - it cannot have been easy. Inevitably she made a huge success of it and was soon representing more companies than she could comfortably cope with.

"I remember being in a New York shop one day when I first spotted the book Glorious Knitting by someone called Kaffe Fassett. I was knocked out by it. I bought six copies - at the full retail price - to give to all my nearest and dearest. The next day I got a call from Rowan asking me to become their representative in The States. I knew of Kaffe's involvement with Rowan and of their wonderful yarns. I had promised myself not to take on any more - but I couldn't resist that one."

Shortly after she was off accompanying Kaffe on a promotional tour of book signings across America. "We hit it off immediately and became firm friends. I just love his approach to design; his attitude of ignoring all the rules, enjoying real colour and that if anything is worth doing its worth over doing. I love that. "

"I had been warned before I met Liza that she talked a lot – and she does!"
Kaffe remembers affectionately, . . .

"I had been warned before I met Liza that she talked a lot – and she does!" Kaffe remembers affectionately, " but that was from the start more of a pleasure than a burden. She's as bright as a penny with such a quick intelligence. I'm lucky to work with someone who has such a respect and real understanding of what I do. We work well together."

By now Liza had married her husband's best friend Drew, a Software Engineer, who had been a huge support to her through the tough years. They live in a clapboard house in New Hope with their two daughters Alexandra, 12, and Elizabeth, 8, a British bulldog called Delilah, a garden filled with English cottage flowers and vegetables and a very efficient fence to keep out the hordes of scavenger deer that roam that area of Pennsylvania.

"I'd got enthusiastic about patchwork and quilting when I was pregnant with Alexandra. Kaffe had never done any patchwork but I thought he would be brilliant – so I sent him a postcard one day saying something flip like 'Hiya Honey – wanna do a patchwork book?' He sent back a vague reply. I could tell he wasn't keen. So I made a patchwork of 'Pennants', one of his knitwear designs, to show him that, at heart, he was really a quilter.

Although Kaffe appreciated that traditional patchwork had influenced his work tremendously he was not particularly interested in achieving the art form himself. " I thought it was all about old clothes and cutting them up" he admits , with a laugh "and I couldn't see how it would work for a book. But Liza said I was so wrong and that we would use new fabrics and then she proceeded to bombard me with blocks and ideas through the post. By the fourth one I started correcting her blocks and sending them back." He was hooked.

"You could say I wore him down," said Liza. Anyway they were off on a collaboration that resulted in the Glorious Patchwork book. A year after that she convinced

Above: Liza and Kaffe working on their latest projects

... "but that was from the start more of a pleasure than a burden. She's as bright as a penny with such a quick intelligence. "

Photography: Drew Lucy

Stephen Sheard of Rowan that they must do a magazine "that would do the same for patchwork that Rowan had done for knitting – modern ideas and great design " said Liza. "Its entirely due to her that we made a move into patchwork" said Stephen. Happily all this coincided with a project Kaffe had done for Oxfam. In 1976 he had been asked to visit villages in India to advise on fabric designs that could be marketed in The West as shirts and bedcovers. Initially a lack of looms and any effective marketing threatened oblivion for the whole project. But gradually it dawned on everyone that these fabrics would be perfect for patchwork and the link between the patchwork books and the Indian weavers turned into another success story with all the humanitarian and environmental elements to delight Liza.

Practically it is one of the unique strengths of the magazine that any reader can actually produce one of the designs in the exact fabrics shown, switching colour ways if they wish.

While Liza has contributed her own designs to the magazine from the start and there are four more in this issue, she and Kaffe are still very active patchwork collaborators. "She is a fantastic teacher in the workshops we do, much better than me" said Kaffe " She's very clear and communicates the boundaries, ideas and short cuts with such a juicy, imaginative choice of words that people can understand immediately and make it work for themselves."

Their patchworking sessions together are notorious for a kind of musical accompaniment. "We are both dotty about the theatre and musical comedies and we love to sing songs from Show Boat or Kiss me Kate or old Beatles numbers. As we're both tone deaf – the sound is appalling. But when you are working with small fiddly bits of fabric its a great way to ease tension."

I don't know what you think but Liza Prior Lucy sounds a remarkable woman and a heck of a lot of fun .

Above: Liza with daughters Alexandra and Elizabeth, bulldog Delilah and guinea pigs Annie and Maggie

Attic Windows

KAFFE FASSETT

I love the crispness of this layout and feel the way it shows off my new fabrics is a treat.

SIZE OF QUILT
The finished quilt will measure approx. 74in x 86in (188cm x 218cm).

MATERIALS
Patchwork fabrics:

FLORAL DANCE

Blue	GP12-B:	¼yd (23cm)
Magenta	GP12-MG:	¼yd (23cm)
Ochre	GP12-O:	¼yd (23cm)
Pink	GP12-P:	¼yd (23cm)
Mauve	GP12-MV:	¼yd (23cm)

ROMAN GLASS

Red	GP01-R:	¼yd (23cm)
Leafy	GP01-L:	¼yd (23cm)
Stones	GP01-S:	¼yd (23cm)
Gold	GP01-G:	¼yd (23cm)

DAMASK

Pastel	GP02-P:	¼yd (23cm)
Jewel	GP02-J:	¼yd (23cm)

ARTICHOKES

Leafy	GP07-L:	¼yd (23cm)
Jewel	GP07-J:	¼yd (23cm)
Stones	GP07-S:	¼yd (23cm)

FORGET-ME-NOT-ROSES

Jewel	GP08-J:	¼yd (23cm)

SHOT COTTON

Sage	SC 17:	½yd (45cm)
Lichen	SC 19:	¼yd (23cm)
Putty	SC 29:	½yd (45cm)
Mushroom	SC 31:	½yd (45cm)

CHRYSANTHEMUM

Ochre	GP13-O:	¼yd (23cm)
Red	GP13-R:	See borders
Blue	GP13-B:	¼yd (23cm)
Green	GP13-G:	See borders

DOTTY

Lavender	GP14-L:	¼yd (23cm)
Terracotta	GP14-T:	¼yd (23cm)
Ochre	GP14-O:	¼yd (23cm)
Sea Green	GP14-SG:	¼yd (23cm)
Plum	GP14-P:	¼yd (23cm)
Cobalt	GP14-C:	¼yd (23cm)
Driftwood	GP14-D:	¼yd (23cm)

BUBBLES

Grey	GP15-G:	¼yd (23cm)
Cobalt	GP15-C:	¼yd (23cm)
Ochre	GP15-O:	¼yd (23cm)
Sky Blue	GP15-S:	¼yd (23cm)
Plum	GP15-P:	See binding

Border fabrics:

CHRYSANTHEMUM

Red	GP13-R:	⅞yd (80cm)
Green	GP13-GN:	⅞yd (80cm)

ROWAN STRIPE

	RS 04:	½yd (45cm)
	RS 07:	½yd (45cm)

Backing fabric:

SHOT COTTON

Lichen	SC 19:	4⅜yds (4.00m)

Binding fabric:

BUBBLES

Plum	GP15-P:	¾ yd (70cm)

Batting:
79in x 90in (200cm by 230cm).

Quilting thread:
Dull Green machine quilting thread.

Templates:
See page 97

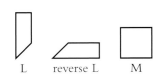

Quilt assembly

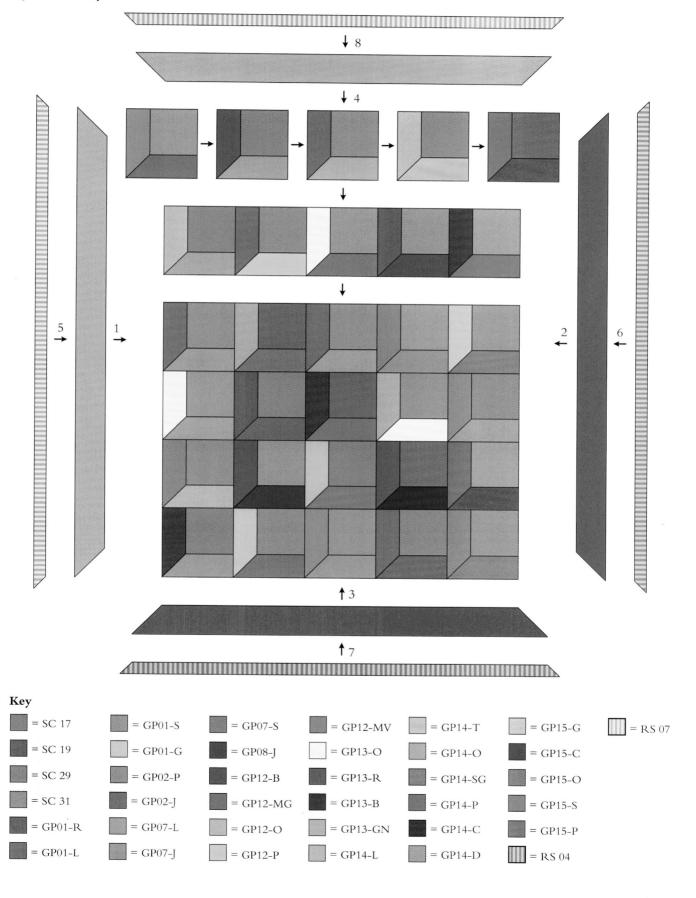

Key

= SC 17	= GP01-S	= GP07-S	= GP12-MV	= GP14-T	= GP15-G	= RS 07
= SC 19	= GP01-G	= GP08-J	= GP13-O	= GP14-O	= GP15-C	
= SC 29	= GP02-P	= GP12-B	= GP13-R	= GP14-SG	= GP15-O	
= SC 31	= GP02-J	= GP12-MG	= GP13-B	= GP14-P	= GP15-S	
= GP01-R	= GP07-L	= GP12-O	= GP13-GN	= GP14-C	= GP15-P	
= GP01-L	= GP07-J	= GP12-P	= GP14-L	= GP14-D	= RS 04	

PATCH SHAPES

The quilt centre is made up one square patch shape and one trapezium patch shape for the left side of each block which is reversed for the bottom of each block. The templates for this quilt as printed at 50% of true size. Photocopy at 200% before using.

CUTTING OUT

Template L: Cut 4½in- (11.5cm-) wide strips across the width of the fabric. Each strip will give you 3 patches per 45in- (114cm-) wide fabric.
Cut 4 in GP12-MG, GP12-MV, 3 in GP02-J, GP12-B, GP13-B, 2 in GP02-P, GP12-O, GP12-P, GP13-O, GP13-R, GP13-GN, 1 in GP15-G.

Template reverse L: Cut 4½in- (11.5cm-) wide strips across the width of the fabric. Each strip will give you 3 patches per 45in- (114cm-) wide fabric.
Cut 3 in GP14-D, GP15-S, 2 in GP01-R, GP01-L, GP07-J, GP14-O, GP14-SG, 1 in GP01-S, GP01-G, GP07-L, GP07-S, GP08-J, GP13-O, GP14-L, GP14-T, GP14-P, GP14-C, GP15-G, GP15-C, GP15-O, GP15-P.

Template M: Cut 8½in- (21.5cm-) wide strips across the width of the fabric. Each strip will give you 5 patches per 45in- (114cm-) wide fabric.
Cut 10 in SC 29, 8 in SC 17, SC 31, 4 in SC 19.

Borders: For inner borders cut 4 x 5½in strips   (14cm-) x width of fabric from GP13-R and 4 from GP13-GN. For outer borders cut 4 x 2½in strips (6.5cm-) x width of fabric from RS 04 and 4 from RS 07.

Binding: cut 8 strips 2¼in- (6.cm-) wide x width of fabric in GP15-C.

Backing: Cut 2 pieces, 78½in x 45in (200cm by 114cm).

MAKING THE BLOCKS

Using a ¼in (6mm) seam allowance throughout, make up 30 blocks using the block and quilt assembly diagrams as a guide. Start by joining the two trapezium patch shapes (templates L and reverse L) along the diagonal edge. Then, using the inset seam technique (see page 102) add the square patch shape (template M).

Block assembly

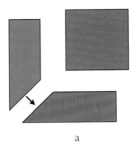

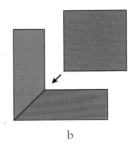

a

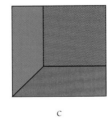

b

c

MAKING UP THE ROWS

Assemble 6 rows of 5 blocks, use the quilt assembly diagram as a guide.

MAKING UP AND ADDING THE BORDERS

For the borders take pairs of strips of the same fabric and join using a ¼in (6mm) seam allowance.

For the side inner borders cut 1 strip 84in x 5½in (211cm x 14cm) from GP13-R and 1 from GP13-GN. For the top and bottom inner borders cut 1 strip 72in x 5½in (180.5cm x 14cm) from GP13-R and 1 from GP13-GN.

For the side outer borders cut 1 strip 88in x 2½in (221cm x 6.5cm) from RS 04 and 1 from RS 07. For the top and bottom outer borders cut 1 strip 76in x 2½in (190.5cm x 6.5cm) from RS 04 and 1 from RS 07.

The borders are generously cut so that the corners can be mitred (See Mitreing Borders on page 105).

Join the inner borders in the order indicated by the quilt assembly diagram, mitre the corners and then add the outer borders and repeat the mitreing process.

FINISHING THE QUILT

Press the quilt top. Seam the backing pieces using a ¼in (6mm) seam allowance to form a piece 78½in x 89.5in (200cm x 227cm) Layer the quilt top, batting and backing and baste together (see page 105). Using dull green machine quilting thread stitch a giant meander pattern across the whole quilt. Trim the quilt edges and attach the binding (see page 106).

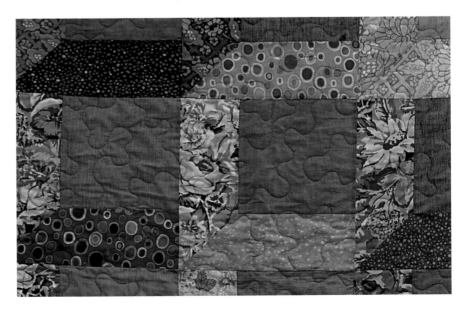

Amish Cushions ★/★★

LIZA PRIOR LUCY

CUTTING OUT
Cushion front:
Template VV: Cut 4 in SC 37.
Cut 1 Square 7½in x 7½in (19cm x 19cm) in SC 14.
Cut 4 squares 1½in x 1½in (3.75cm x 3.75cm) in SC 39.
Cut 4 strips 1½in x 10½in (3.75cm x 26.5cm) in SC 36.
Cut 4 strips 3½in x 12½in (9cm x 31.75cm) in SC 29.
Cut 4 squares 3½in x 3½in (9cm x 9cm) in SC 14.
Cushion back:
Cut 1 piece18½in x 15½in (47cm x 39.5cm) and 1 piece 18½in x 11in (47cm x 28cm) in SC 36.

MAKING THE DIAMOND IN A SQUARE CUSHION

Using a ¼ in (6mm) seam allowance throughout, make up the cushion centre as shown in the diagrams, then add the borders as for the Bars cushion.

Liza has used traditional Amish design with modern colours to create a collection of cushions which will look good in a contemporary setting.

Block assembly

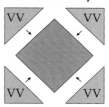

SIZE OF CUSHIONS
The finished cushions will measure approx. 18in x 18in (46cm x 46cm).

Templates:
See page 86

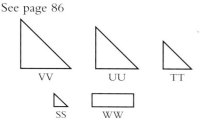

PATCH SHAPES
The three cushions are made up using four sizes of triangle (templates SS, TT, UU and VV) one odd sized rectangle

for which a template is provided (template WW) and a variety of other rectangles and squares, cut at easily measured sizes.

Diamond in a Square Cushion ★
MATERIALS
Patchwork Fabrics:
SHOT COTTON
Lavender	SC 14:	¼yd (23cm)
Putty	SC 29:	⅛yd (15cm)
Lilac	SC 36:	⅔yd (60cm)

cushion back included.
Coffee	SC 37:	¼yd (23cm)
Apple	SC 39:	⅛yd (15cm)

Cushion assembly

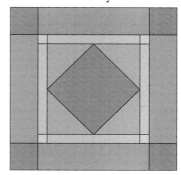

Key

= SC 29   = SC 36
= SC 14   = SC 37
= SC 39

Bars Cushion

MATERIALS
Patchwork Fabrics:

SHOT COTTON

Lavender	SC 14:	$\frac{1}{2}$yd (45cm)

cushion back included.

Putty	SC 29:	$\frac{1}{8}$yd (15cm)
Lilac	SC 36:	$\frac{1}{8}$yd (15cm)
Coffee	SC 37:	$\frac{1}{8}$yd (15cm)
Apple	SC 39:	$\frac{1}{8}$yd (15cm)

CUTTING OUT
Cushion front:

Cut 3 strips 2$\frac{1}{2}$in x 10$\frac{1}{2}$in (6.5cm x 26.5cm) in SC 39.

Cut 2 strips 2$\frac{1}{2}$in x 10$\frac{1}{2}$in (6.5cm x 26.5cm) in SC 29.

Cut 4 squares 1$\frac{1}{2}$in x 1$\frac{1}{2}$in (3.75cm x 3.75cm) in SC 29.

★ Cut 4 strips 1$\frac{1}{2}$in x 10$\frac{1}{2}$in (3.75cm x 26.5cm) in SC 14.

Cut 4 strips 3$\frac{1}{2}$in x 12$\frac{1}{2}$in (9cm x 31.75cm) in SC 37.

Cut 4 squares 3$\frac{1}{2}$in x 3$\frac{1}{2}$in (9cm x 9cm) in SC 36.

Cushion back:

Cut 1 piece18$\frac{1}{2}$in x 15$\frac{1}{2}$in (47cm x 39.5cm) and 1 piece 18$\frac{1}{2}$in x 11in (47cm x 28cm) in SC 14

MAKING THE BARS CUSHION

Using a $\frac{1}{4}$in (6mm) seam allowance throughout, make up the cushion centre as shown in the diagrams, then add the borders in the order shown.

Block assembly

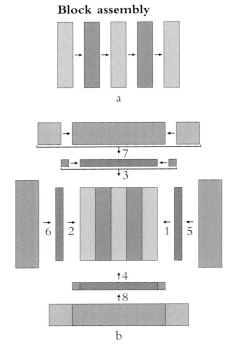

a

b

Cushion assembly

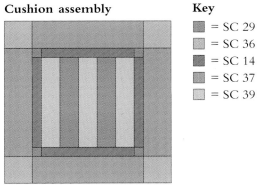

Key

▨	= SC 29
▨	= SC 36
▨	= SC 14
▨	= SC 37
▨	= SC 39

Amish Baskets Cushion ★★

MATERIALS
Patchwork Fabrics:

SHOT COTTON

Lavender	SC 14:	$\frac{1}{8}$yd (15cm)
Putty	SC 29:	$\frac{1}{2}$yd (45cm)

cushion back included.

Lilac	SC 36:	$\frac{1}{8}$yd (15cm)
Coffee	SC 37:	$\frac{1}{4}$yd (23cm)
Apple	SC 39:	$\frac{1}{8}$yd (15cm)

CUTTING OUT
Cushion front:

Template SS: Cut 10 in SC 14, 13 in SC 39 and 2 in SC 37.

Template TT: Cut 1 in SC 39.

Template UU: Cut 1 in SC 37.

Template VV: Cut 4 in SC 29.

Template WW: Cut 2 in SC 39.

Cut 4 squares 1$\frac{1}{2}$in x 1$\frac{1}{2}$in (3.75cm x 3.75cm) in SC 14.

Cut 4 strips 1$\frac{1}{2}$in x 10$\frac{1}{2}$in (3.75cm x 26.5cm) in SC 37.

Cut 4 strips 3$\frac{1}{2}$in x 12$\frac{1}{2}$in (9cm x 31.75cm) in SC 36.

Cut 4 squares 3$\frac{1}{2}$in x 3$\frac{1}{2}$in (9cm x 9cm) in SC 39.

Cushion back:

Cut 1 piece18$\frac{1}{2}$in x 15$\frac{1}{2}$in (47cm x 39.5cm) and 1 piece 18$\frac{1}{2}$in x 11in (47cm x 28cm) in SC 29.

MAKING THE AMISH BASKETS CUSHION

Using a $\frac{1}{4}$in (6mm) seam allowance throughout, make up the cushion centre as shown in the diagrams, then add the borders as for the Bars cushion.

FINISHING THE CUSHIONS

To finish the cushions follow the instruction on page 107.

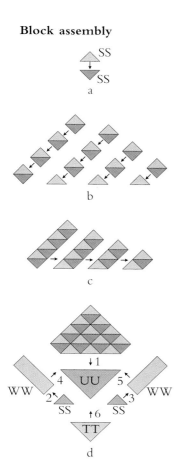

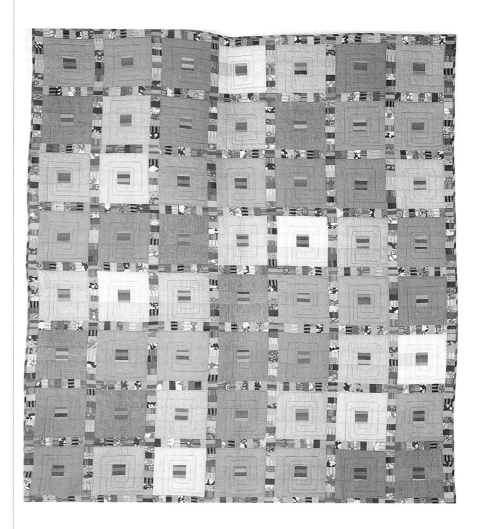

Birdboxes ★★

KAFFE FASSETT

Cushion assembly

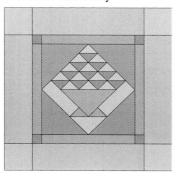

Key

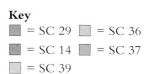

◼ = SC 29   ◻ = SC 36
◼ = SC 14   ◼ = SC 37
◻ = SC 39

C ool blocks in shot cottons bordered by sashing strips in a myriad of lively prints and stripes make this quilt unmistakeably a Kaffe Fassett design. Some of the bright prints in the sashing borders have been subdued by Tea-Dyeing (we tell you how this is done)

SIZE OF QUILT
The finished quilt will measure approx. 77½in x 68in (197cm x 173cm).

MATERIALS
Patchwork Fabrics:
ALTERNATE STRIPE
AS 01: ¼yd (23cm)
EXOTIC STRIPE
ES 21: ¼yd (23cm)

SHOT COTTON

Tangerine	SC 11:	¼yd (23cm)
Chartreuse	SC 12:	¼yd (23cm)
Lavender	SC 14:	½yd (45cm)
Mustard	SC 16:	½yd (45cm)
Sage	SC 17:	½yd (45cm)
Lichen	SC 19:	½yd (45cm)
Ecru	SC 24:	½yd (45cm)
Duck Egg	SC 26:	½yd (45cm)
Mushroom	SC 31:	½yd (45cm)

Quilt Assembly

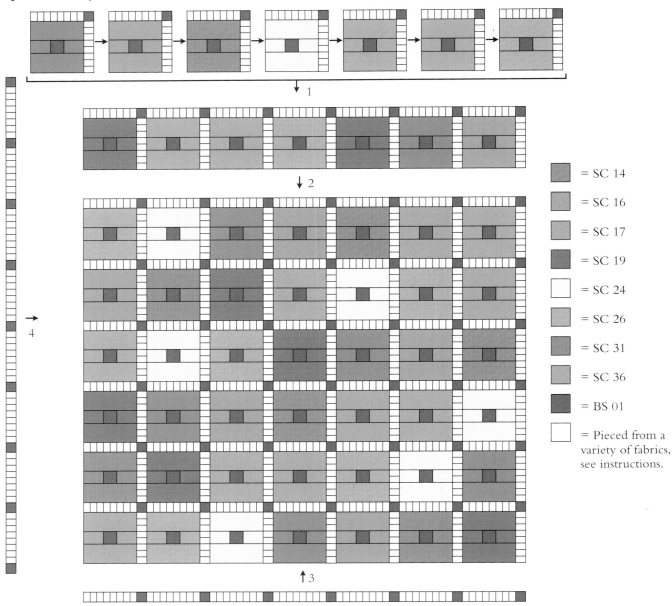

= SC 14

= SC 16

= SC 17

= SC 19

= SC 24

= SC 26

= SC 31

= SC 36

= BS 01

= Pieced from a variety of fabrics, see instructions.

Watermelon	SC 33: ¼yd (23cm)	NARROW STRIPE		**Backing Fabric:**	
Sunshine	SC 35: ¼yd (23cm)		NS 01: ¼yd (23cm)	PRESSED ROSES	
Lilac	SC 36: ½yd (45cm)	PRESSED ROSES			PR 02: 4yds (3.65m)
BROAD STRIPE			PR 02: ¼yd (23cm)	**Bias binding:**	
	BS 01: 1⅛yds (1m)		PR 04: ¼yd (23cm)	BROAD STRIPE	
ROMAN GLASS			PR 05: ¼yd (23cm)		BS 01: see patchwork fabrics
Blue & White	GP01-BW: ¼yd (23cm)		PR 06: ¼yd (23cm)	**Batting:**	
Circus	GP01-C: ¼yd (23cm)	ROWAN STRIPE		82in x 72in	
Gold	GP01-G: ¼yd (23cm)		RS 03: ¼yd (23cm)	**Quilting thread:**	
Red	GP01-R: ¼yd (23cm)		RS 05: ¼yd (23cm)	Machine quilting thread soft grey.	

Templates:
See pages 86 & 95

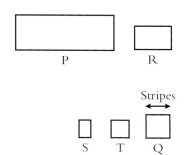

PATCH SHAPES

The blocks are made up of one square shape (template Q) two rectangle shapes (templates R & P). The quilt also has sashing (template S) and sashing posts (template T) (see glossary). The sashing strips are joined to two sides of the blocks for easy assembly of the quilt top.

CUTTING OUT

Template Q: Cut 2½in- (6.5cm-) strips across the width of the fabric. Each strip will give you 17 patches per 45in- (114cm-) wide fabric. Cut 56 in BS 01.
Template P: Cut 3½in- (9cm-) strips across the width of the fabric. Each strip will give you 5 patches per 45in- (114cm-) wide fabric. Cut 14 in SC 14, SC 16, SC 17, SC 19, SC 24, SC 26, SC 31 and SC 36.
Template R: Cut 3½in- (9cm-) strips across the width of the fabric. Cut 14 in SC 14, SC 16, SC 17, SC 19, SC 24, SC 26, SC 31 and SC 36.
Template S: Cut 1½in- (4cm-) strips across the width of the fabric. Each strip will give you 22 patches per 45in- (114cm-) wide fabric. Cut a total of 1016 in the following fabrics, SC 11, SC 12, SC 33, SC 35, GP01-BW, GP01-C, GP01-G, GP01-R, AS 01, ES 21, NS 01, PR 02, PR 04, PR 05, PR 06, RS 03, and RS 05.
Note: An alternative way of making the sashing sections is to cut the 1½in- (4cm-) strips and then join four along the length. Then cut 2in (5cm) slices.
Dont be tempted to sew more than four strips together as the sashing bars will look too regular.
Template T: Cut 2in- (5cm-) strips across the width of the fabric.
Each strip will give you 21 patches per 45in- (114cm-) wide fabric. Cut 72 in BS 01.
Bias binding: Cut 8½yds (7.75m) of 2½in- (6.5cm-) wide bias binding from BS 01.
Backing: Cut 2 pieces 41in by 72in (104cm by 182cm).

Block Assembly

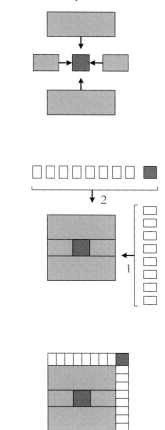

MAKING THE BLOCKS

Using a ¼in (6mm) seam allowance throughout, make up 56 blocks, using the quilt assembly diagram as a guide to fabric placement. Note: the stripe direction for fabric BS 01 is always horizontal. Make 127 sashing bars of 8 patches (template S) choosing fabrics with abrupt colour next to each other.

Join a sashing bar to the right side of each block. Add a sashing post (template T) to 56 sashing bars and join one to the top of each block. Make up two longer sections of sashing for the bottom and side of the quilt as shown in the quilt assembly diagram.

MAKING UP THE ROWS

Assemble 8 rows of 7 blocks, join the rows and then the long sashing sections on the order indicated in the quilt assembly diagram.

FINISHING THE QUILT

Press the quilt top. Seam the two backing pieces together with a ¼in (6mm) seam allowance to form one piece approximately 81in x 72in (205cm x 182cm). Layer the quilt top, batting and backing and baste together (see page 105). Using the soft grey machine quilting thread, quilt square snail shapes in the blocks and a meandering pattern in the sashing as indicated by the quilting diagram. Trim the quilt edges and attach the binding (see page 106). The sashing sections of this quilt were tea-dyed (see page 108) to give them a more subdued effect.

Quilting Diagram

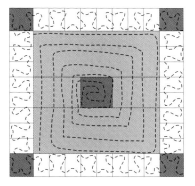

Bobbins Quilt

PAULINE SMITH

T he scraps of fabric and bobbins of thread in her grandmother's workbox were Pauline's inspiration for this simple quilt.

SIZE OF QUILT
The finished quilt will measure approx. 91in x 73in (231cm x 185cm).

MATERIALS
Patchwork Fabrics:
SHOT COTTON

Ecru	SC 24:	½yd (45cm)
Duck Egg	SC 26:	½yd (45cm)
Putty	SC 29:	½yd (45cm)
Lilac	SC 36:	½yd (45cm)

OMBRE STRIPE
	OS 02:	½yd (45cm)
	OS 05:	½yd (45cm) or

cut from leftover backing fabric.

BLUE AND WHITE STRIPE
	BWS01:	½yd (45cm)
	BWS02:	½yd (45cm)

PRESSED ROSES
	PR01:	1yd (90cm)

DAMASK
Pastel	GP02-P:	½yd (45cm)

Stones | GP02-S: ½yd (45cm)
GAZANIA
Stones | GP03-S: ½yd (45cm)
ARTICHOKES
Stones | GP07-S: 1¼yds (115cm)
FORGET-ME-NOT ROSES
Stones | GP08-S: ½yd (45cm)
FLORAL DANCE
Mauve | GP12-M: ½yd (45cm)
DOTTY
Driftwood | GP14-D: ½yd (45cm)
BUBBLES
Grey | GP15-G: ⅔yd (60cm)

Border Fabric:
ARTICHOKES
Stones | GP07-S: see above.

Backing Fabric:
OMBRE STRIPE
| OS 05: 5½yds (5.10m)

Binding Fabric:
PRESSED ROSES
| PR 01: see above.

Batting:
95in x 78in (241cm x 198cm).

Quilting thread:
Toning machine quilting thread.

Templates:
See pages 95 & 96

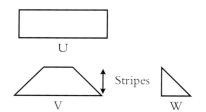

PATCH SHAPES
The quilt centre is made up from blocks of one rectangle (template U), two trapeziums (template V) and four triangles (template W).

CUTTING OUT
Template U: Cut 2½in- (6.5cm-) wide strips across the width of the fabric. Each strip will give you 6 patches per 45in- (114cm-) wide fabric.
Cut 21 in GP15-G, 19 in GP02-P, 18 in GP14-D, 17 in GP08-S, GP07-S, 16 in GP12-M, PR 01, 15 in GP02-S, GP03-S.
Template V: Cut 2½in- (6.5cm-) wide strips across the width of the fabric. Each strip will give you 8 patches per 45in- (114cm-) wide fabric.

Quilt assembly

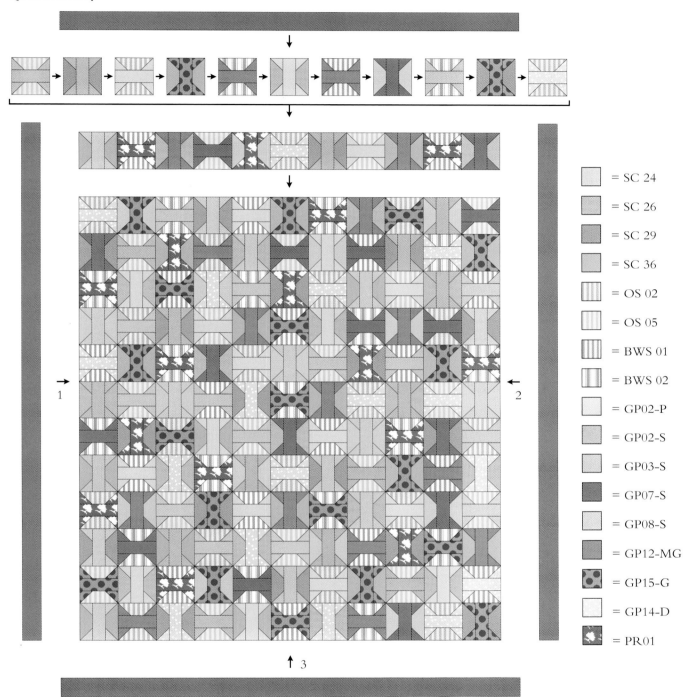

= SC 24
= SC 26
= SC 29
= SC 36
= OS 02
= OS 05
= BWS 01
= BWS 02
= GP02-P
= GP02-S
= GP03-S
= GP07-S
= GP08-S
= GP12-MG
= GP15-G
= GP14-D
= PR01

Cut 40 in OS 02, SC 29, SC 36, 38 in OS 05, BWS01, BWS02, SC 26, 36 in SC 24.

Template W: Cut 3in- (7.5cm-) wide strips across the width of the fabric. Each strip will give you 28 patches per 45in- (114cm-) wide fabric.

Cut 84 in GP15-G, 76 in GP02-P, 72 in GP14-D, 68 in GP08-S, GP07-S, 64 in GP12-M, PR 01, 60 in GP02-S, GP03-S.

Borders: For side borders cut 4 strips 42½in x 3½in (108cm x 9cm) and for top and bottom borders cut 4 strips 36½in x 3½in (93cm x 9cm) in GP07-S.

Binding: cut 8 strips 2in- (5cm-) wide x width of fabric in PR 01.

Backing: Cut 1 piece 97in x 45in (246cm by 114cm) and 1 piece 97in x 33in, (246cm by 84cm).

MAKING THE BLOCKS

Using a ¼in (6mm) seam allowance throughout, make up 154 blocks, use quilt and block assembly diagrams as a guide.

Box Cars

KAFFE FASSETT

Block assembly

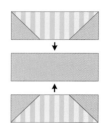

a

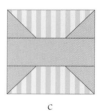

b

c

MAKING UP THE ROWS
Assemble 14 rows of 11 blocks, use the quilt assembly diagram as a guide.

MAKING THE BORDERS
Join the side border strips to form 2 strips 84½in x 3½in (214.5cm x 9cm). Join the top and bottom border strips to form 2 strips 72½in x 3½in (184cm x 9cm) Add the borders to the quilt centre in the order indicated by the quilt assembly diagram.

FINISHING THE QUILT
Press the quilt top. Seam the backing pieces using a ¼in (6mm) seam allowance to form a piece 97in x 77½in (246cm by 197cm). Layer the quilt top, batting and backing and baste together (see page 105). Using a toning thread, stitch-in-the-ditch along the seam lines, between the blocks and along each border. Trim the quilt edges and attach the binding (see page106).

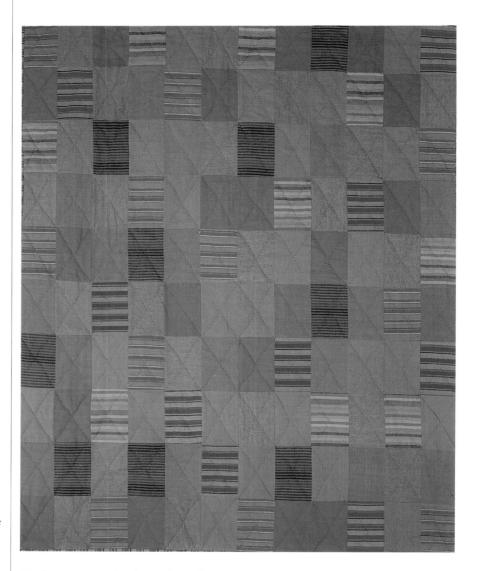

Ports stacked with red containers have always attracted my eye. This red on red study has just been waiting to happen. Kaffe has used an oblong block, careful placing of colour and simple hand quilting, to create this intensely coloured quilt.

SIZE OF QUILT
The finished quilt will measure approx. 75in x 60in (190cm x 152cm).

MATERIALS
Patchwork fabrics:

SHOT COTTON

Ginger	SC 01:	¾yd (70cm)
Persimmon	SC 07:	⅞yd (80cm)
Raspberry	SC 08:	⅞yd (80cm)
Bittersweet	SC 10:	¾yd (70cm)

NARROW STRIPE
  NS 01: ⅜yd (35cm)
ALTERNATE STRIPE
  AS 03: ½yd (45cm) or use the leftovers from the backing
  AS 10: ⅜yd (35cm)
PACHRANGI STRIPE
  PS 05: ⅜yd (35cm)
Backing Fabric:
ALTERNATE STRIPE
  AS 03: 3½yds (3.2m)

Quilt assembly

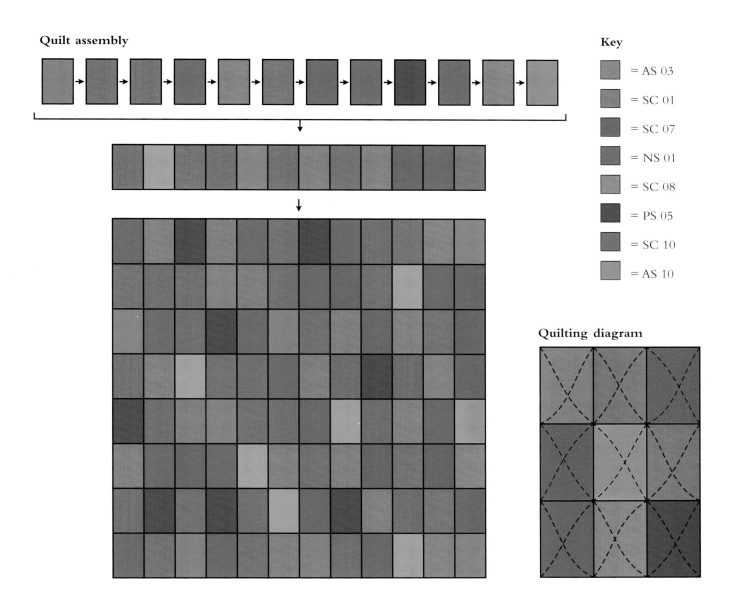

Key

= AS 03
= SC 01
= SC 07
= NS 01
= SC 08
= PS 05
= SC 10
= AS 10

Quilting diagram

Straight cut binding:
ALTERNATE STRIPE
        AS 10: ⅝yd (50cm)
Batting:
80in x 65in
Quilting thread:
Perlé cotton in burnt orange

Template:
See page 97

Stripes

B

PATCH SHAPE
The quilt is made from one rectangle patch shape.

CUTTING OUT
Template B: Cut 5½in- (14cm-) wide strips across the width of the fabric. Each strip will give you 5 patches per 45in- (114cm-) wide fabric.
Cut 23 in SC 07, 21 in SC 08, 20 in SC 01, 18 in SC 10, 11 in AS 03, 9 in NS 01, 9 in AS 10, 9 in PS 05.
Backing:
Cut 1 piece 45in x 63in (114cm x 160cm) and 1 piece 35in x 63in (90cm x 160cm).
Binding:
Cut 7 strips 2½in- (6.5cm-) x width of fabric in AS10, to form 7¾yds (7m) of binding.

MAKING THE QUILT
Using a ¼in (6mm) seam allowance,

assemble 10 rows of 12 patches (template B). Use the quilt assembly diagram as a guide. Join the rows to form the quilt top.

FINISHING THE QUILT
Press the assembled quilt top. Seam the two backing pieces together with a ¼in (6mm) seam allowance to form one piece approximately 80in x 63in (203cm x 160cm).
Layer the quilt top, batting and backing and baste together (see page 105).
Using the perlé thread quilt in a rustic style grid as shown in the quilting diagram.
Trim the quilt edges and attach the binding (see page 106).

Casbah

PAULINE SMITH

The rich palette of Henri Matissse's Moroccan Paintings inspired the fabric selection in this colourful quilt. Gentle, earthy colours would also look good.

SIZE OF QUILT

The finished quilt will measure approx. 79½in x 97½in (202cm x 248cm).

MATERIALS

Patchwork Fabrics:

SHOT COTTON
Navy   SC 13: 1¼yd (1.15m)
Duck Egg   SC 26: 1yd (90cm)
Pine   SC 21: 1yd (90cm)

BROAD STRIPE
              BS 08: 1¼yd (1.15m)
PACHRANGI STRIPE
              PS 01: ½yd (45cm)
NARROW STRIPE
              NS 01: 1yd (90cm)
BROAD STRIPE
              BS 11: ½yd (45cm)
              BS 01: 1yd (90cm)
ALTERNATE STRIPE
              AS 03: ½yd (45cm)

Border Fabric:

SHOT COTTON
Persimmon   SC 07: 2½yds (2.3m)

Backing Fabric:
BROAD STRIPE
              BS 01: 5⅝yds (5.15m)

Bias binding:
PACHRANGI STRIPE
              PS 01: ½yd (45cm)

Batting:
82in x 100in

Quilting thread:
Hand quilting thread in burnt orange.

Templates:
See page 91

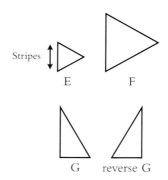

PATCH SHAPES

The quilt centre is made up of two sizes of equilateral triangles. The smaller triangles (template E) are pieced into blocks and then alternated with the larger triangles (template F) to form the quilt rows with a third triangle shape to fill in at the row ends (template G and reverse G). You'll find half template F on page 91 Place edge of template F to fold of paper. Trace around shape and cut out from double thickness paper. Open out for the complete template.

CUTTING OUT

Template E: Cut 4¼in- (10.7cm-) strips along the length of the fabric. Cut 132 in BS 08, 99 in NS 01 and BS 01, cut 44 in PS01, 33 in BS11 and AS 03, .

Template F: Cut 7¾in- (19.5cm-) strips across the width of the fabric. Each strip will give you 9 patches per 45in- (114cm-) wide fabric. Cut 40 in SC 13, 30 in SC 21 and SC26.

Quilt assembly

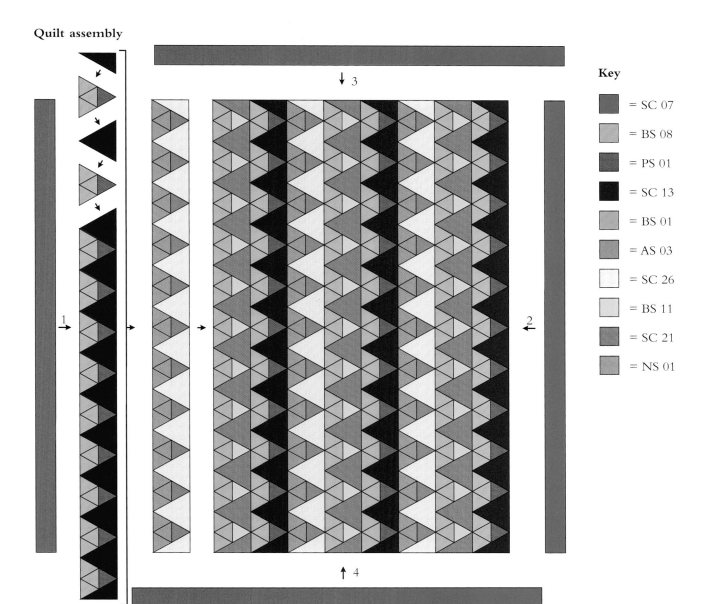

Key

= SC 07

= BS 08

= PS 01

= SC 13

= BS 01

= AS 03

= SC 26

= BS 11

= SC 21

= NS 01

Template G and reverse G: Using the leftovers from cutting template F shapes, cut 4 in SC 13, 3 in SC 21 and SC26, then flip the template over and cut 4 in SC 13, 3 in SC 21 and SC26.

Borders: Cut 2 side border strips 5in (12.5cm) by 88½in (225cm) and 2 end border strips 5in (12.5cm) by 80in (203cm)

Binding: Cut 10yds (9m) of 2½in- (6.5cm-) wide bias binding from PS 01.

Backing: Cut 2 pieces 45in by 101in (114cm by 256cm).

Block assembly

a

b

Beasties Cushion

PAULINE SMITH

MAKING THE BLOCKS

Using a ¹⁄₄in (6mm) seam allowance throughout, make up 110 blocks, using the quilt assembly diagram as a guide to fabric placement. The stripe direction is indicated by the block diagram.

MAKING UP THE ROWS

Assemble 10 rows alternating the pieced blocks with the large triangles (template F) using the quilt assembly diagram as a guide. The ends of each row are filled using the half triangles (template G and Reverse G)

ADDING THE OUTER BORDERS

Add the outer borders in the order indicated by the quilt assembly diagram.

FINISHING THE QUILT

Press the quilt top. Seam the two backing pieces together with a ¹⁄₄in (6mm) seam allowance to form one piece approximately 88in x 101in (224cm x 256cm). Layer the quilt top, batting and backing and baste together (see page 105). Using the toning hand quilting thread, quilt as indicated by the quilting diagram. Trim the quilt edges and attach the binding (see page 106).

Quilting diagram

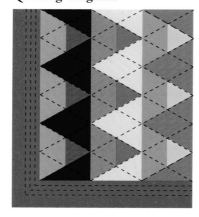

The beasties are appliquéd by hand onto a patchwork background. Pauline used embroidery stitches (french knots and running stitches) to embellish the beasties and suggest the ground on which they stand.

SIZE OF CUSHION

The finished cushion will measure approx.18¹⁄₂ in x 18¹⁄₂ in (47cm x 47cm).

MATERIALS
Patchwork fabrics:
SHOT COTTON
Apple   SC 39: ¹⁄₄yd (23cm)
Cobalt   SC 40: ¹⁄₂yd (45cm)
cushion back included
ROWAN STRIPE
                 RS 02: ¹⁄₂yd (45cm)
cushion back included

Appliqué fabrics:
SHOT COTTON
Opal   SC 05: ¹⁄₈yd (15cm)
Watermelon   SC 33: ¹⁄₈yd (15cm)
Apple   SC 39: use leftovers from
patchwork
FORGET-ME-NOT ROSE
Circus   GP08-C: ¹⁄₈yd (15cm)
FLORAL DANCE
Blue   GP12-B: ¹⁄₈yd (15cm)
ROWAN STRIPE
                 RS 02: use leftovers
from patchwork

Lining:
19in x 19in (48cm x 48cm)
Batting:
19in x 19in (48cm x 48cm)
Embellishing thread:
Stranded cotton in coral, pink, purple, lime green, and turquoise.

Templates:
See page 100

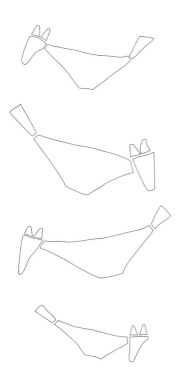

Quilt assembly

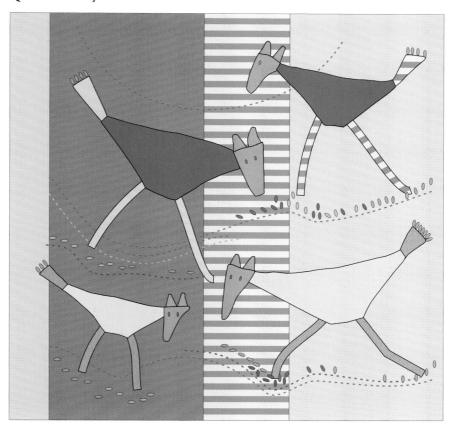

Key

 = SC 05   = SC 39   = RS 02   = GP12-B

= SC 33   = SC 40   = GP08-C

PATCH SHAPES
The cushion is made using rectangles of fabric cut at easily measured sizes, with appliquéd motifs.

CUTTING OUT
Cushion front:
Cut 1 piece 7¼in x 19in (18.5cm x 48cm) in SC 39 and SC 40
Cut 1 piece 4in x 19in (10cm x 48cm) in RS 02
Cut 1 piece 2¼in x 19in (5.5cm x 48cm) in SC 39
Cushion back:
Cut 1 piece 19in x 11in (48cm x 28cm) in SC 40
Cut 1 piece 19in x 13in (48cm x 33cm) in RS 02.

Appliqué shapes: Remember to add a ¼in seam allowance around all appliqué templates. The appliqué templates for this project are printed at 50% of true size. Photocopy at 200% before using.

Cut appliqué shapes in the fabrics indicated on the layout diagram.
Bias cut 8 legs 5in x ¾in (13cm x 2cm) in the fabrics indicated on the layout diagram

MAKING THE CUSHION FRONT
Using a ¼in (6mm) seam allowance throughout, join the four front pieces as shown in the layout diagram.

APPLIQUÉ
Position the appliqué shapes as shown in the layout diagram. Hand appliqué the shapes into place. Layer legs and tails under bodies, the ears next and finally the heads on top (see hand appliqué on page 104).

EMBELLISHING
Layer cushion front, batting and lining and baste together (see page xx). Embellish the cushion front with embroidery stitches as indicated in the diagram, ensuring stitches are carried through batting and lining to secure layers together.

FINISHING THE CUSHION
To finish the cushions follow the instruction on page 107.

Hazy Sunshine

MARY MASHUTA

★★

Templates:
See page 92

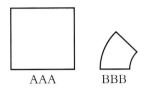

AAA   BBB

PATCH SHAPES

The quilt centre is made up from blocks of one square (template AAA) and one curved segment (template BBB) which are pieced together and then appliquéd to the pieced background rows.

CUTTING OUT

Template AAA: Cut 7½in- (19cm-) wide strips across the width of the fabric. Each strip will give you 5 patches per 45in- (114cm-) wide fabric.
Cut 27 in RS 01, RS 04, RS 07.

Template BBB: Cut 5in- (12.5cm-) wide strips across the width of the fabric. Each strip will give you 9 patches per 45in- (114cm-) wide fabric.
Cut 27 in GP01-G, GP01-S, GP14-D, GP14-O, GP15-G and GP15-O.

Binding: cut 6 strips 2in- (5cm-) wide x width of fabric in SC 18.

Backing Cut 1 piece 67in x 45in (170cm by 114cm) and 1 piece 67in x 23in, (170cm by 59cm).

MAKING QUILT TOP

This quilt is made up in an unusual but very easy way. Using a ¼ in (6mm) seam allowance throughout, piece the 7½" (19cm) squares into rows of 9 blocks, following the layout diagram for fabric placement and stripe direction. Number the rows for easy identification. Piece the appliqué segments into pairs and fours in the colour sequence indicated by the layout diagram. Appliqué the segments to the rows as described in the machine appliqué section (see page 104).

MAKING UP THE ROWS

Assemble the rows, use the quilt assembly diagram as a guide.

Simple, striped blocks placed in a regular pattern form the background onto which the segment shapes, cut from a selection of soft gold, green and grey prints, are appliquéd. Tricky piecing is avoided by the use of appliqué.

SIZE OF QUILT
The finished quilt will measure approx. 63in x 63in (160cm x 160cm).

MATERIALS
Patchwork Fabrics:
ROMAN GLASS
Gold   GP01-G: ½yd (45cm)
Stone   GP01-S: ½yd (45cm)
DOTTY
Driftwood   GP14-D: ½yd (45cm)
Ochre   GP14-O: ½yd (45cm)
BUBBLES
Grey   GP15-G: ½yd (45cm)
Ochre   GP15-O: ½yd (45cm)

ROWAN STRIPE
    RS 01: 1½yds (1.3m)
    RS 04: 1½yds (1.3m)
    RS 07: 1½yds (1.3m)

Backing Fabric:
ROWAN STRIPE
    RS 07: 3¾yds (3.4m)

Binding Fabric:
SHOT COTTON
Tobacco   SC 18: ½yd (45cm)

Batting:
67in x 67in (170cm x 170cm).

Quilting thread:
Machine quilting thread in suitable dark beige.

Quilt assembly

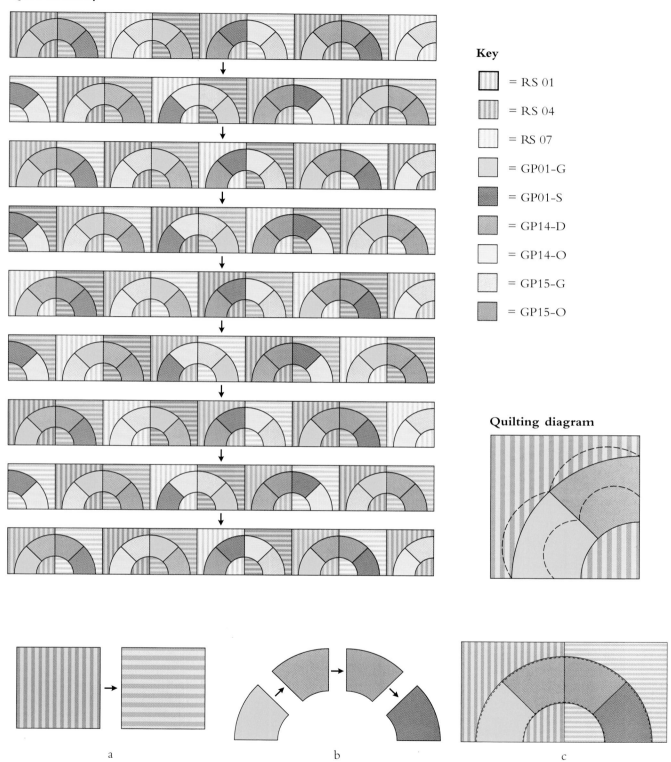

Key

☐ = RS 01

☐ = RS 04

☐ = RS 07

☐ = GP01-G

☐ = GP01-S

☐ = GP14-D

☐ = GP14-O

☐ = GP15-G

☐ = GP15-O

Quilting diagram

a

b

c

FINISHING THE QUILT

Press the quilt top. Seam the backing pieces using a ¼in (6mm) seam allowance to form a piece 67in x 67in (170cm by 170cm). Layer the quilt top, batting and backing and baste together (see page 105). Using the dark beige quilting thread, stitch-in-the-ditch along the seam lines between the blocks and in the pattern shown in the quilting diagram. Trim the quilt edges and attach the binding (see page 106).

Hundreds and Thousands

ELEANOR YATES

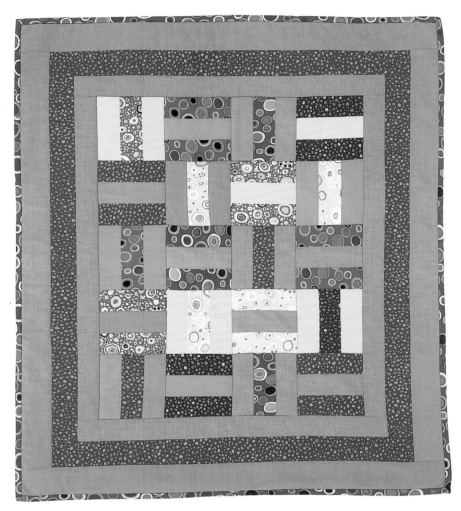

Eleanor chose a vibrant selection of colours for this little pram quilt. A perfect project for a beginner and just the thing to catch a baby's eye.

SIZE OF QUILT

The finished quilt will measure approx. 33½in x 28½in (85cm x 72.5cm).

MATERIALS

Patchwork, Border and Binding Fabrics:

ROMAN GLASS

Leafy	GP01-L:	⅛yd (15cm)
Pastel	GP01-P:	⅛yd (15cm)

SHOT COTTON

Watermelon	SC 33:	⅛yd (15cm)
Lemon	SC 34:	⅛yd (15cm)
Cobalt	SC 40:	⅛yd (15cm)
Jade	SC 41:	¼yd (23cm)
Lime	SC 43:	⅓yd (30cm)

DOTTY

Cobalt	GP14-C:	⅓yd (30cm)
Plum	GP14-P:	⅛yd (15cm)

BUBBLES

Cobalt	GP15-C:	⅓yd (30cm)
Plum	GP15-P:	⅛yd (15cm)

Backing Fabric:

SHOT COTTON

Opal	SC 05:	1yd (90cm)

Batting:
36in x 33in (90cm by 85cm)

Quilting thread:
Toning machine quilting thread.

Template:
See page 90

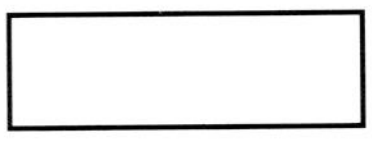

K

PATCH SHAPES

The quilt centre is made up one rectangular patch shape.

CUTTING OUT

Template K: Cut 2in- (5cm-) wide strips across the width of the fabric. Each strip will give you 8 patches per 45in- (114cm-) wide fabric.
Cut 8 in SC 34, 7 in SC 43, 6 in SC 33, SC 41 and GP14-C, 5 in GP01-L, GP01-P, GP14-P and GP15-P, 4 in GP15-C, and 3 in SC 40.

Borders: For the inner borders cut 2 side borders 23in x 2in (58.5cm x 5cm) and two end borders 21½in x 2in (54.5cm x 5cm) in SC 41. For the middle borders cut 2 side borders 26in x 2¼in (66cm x 5.75cm) and two end borders 25in x 2¼in (63.5cm x 5.75cm) in GP14-C. For the outer borders cut 2 side borders 29½in x 2½in (75cm x 6.25cm) and two end borders 29in x 2½in (73.5cm x 6.25cm) in SC 43.

Binding: cut 4 strips 2¼in- (6.cm-) wide x width of fabric in GP15-C.

Backing: Cut 1 piece, 36in x 33in (90cm by 85cm).

MAKING THE BLOCKS

Using a ¼in (6mm) seam allowance throughout, make up 20 blocks, use the quilt assembly diagram as a guide to fabric placement.

Block assembly

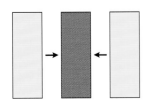

Quilt assembly

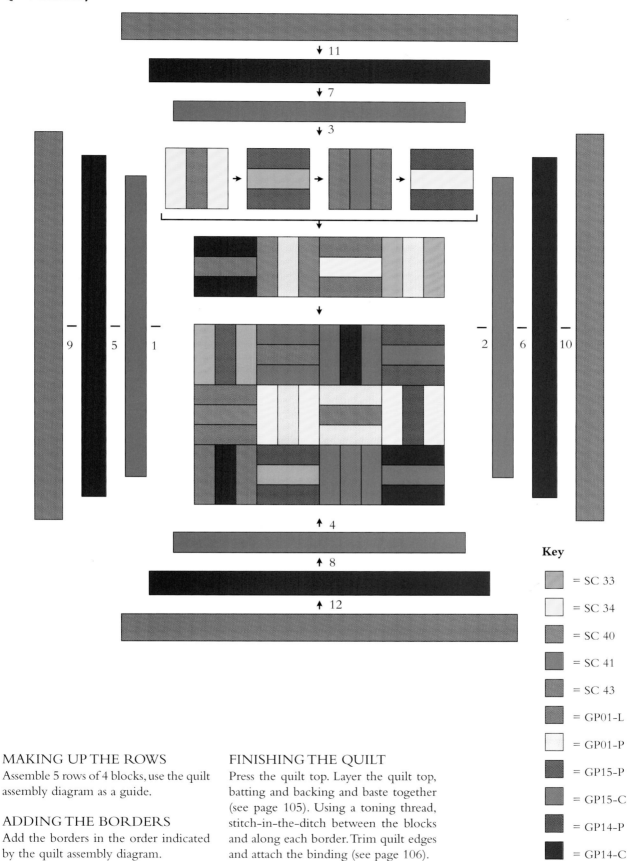

MAKING UP THE ROWS
Assemble 5 rows of 4 blocks, use the quilt assembly diagram as a guide.

ADDING THE BORDERS
Add the borders in the order indicated by the quilt assembly diagram.

FINISHING THE QUILT
Press the quilt top. Layer the quilt top, batting and backing and baste together (see page 105). Using a toning thread, stitch-in-the-ditch between the blocks and along each border. Trim quilt edges and attach the binding (see page 106).

Key

= SC 33
= SC 34
= SC 40
= SC 41
= SC 43
= GP01-L
= GP01-P
= GP15-P
= GP15-C
= GP14-P
= GP14-C

Little Bottles

KAFFE FASSETT

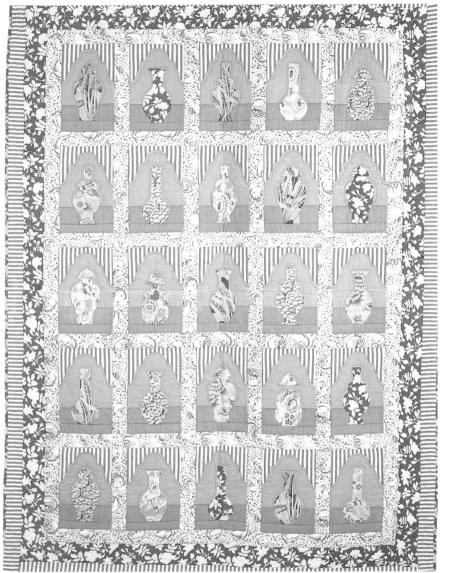

SIZE OF QUILT

The finished quilt will measure approx. 57½ x 80in (146cm x 203cm).

MATERIALS

Patchwork, sashing and border fabrics:

ROWAN STRIPE
08   RS 08: 1½yds (1.35m)
SHOT COTTON
Ecru   SC 24: 1⅜yd (1.25m)
Putty   SC 29: ½yd (45cm)
PRESSED ROSES
01   PR 01: 1yd (90cm)
DAMASK
Circus   GP02-C: ¼yd (23cm)
Pastel   GP02-P: ¼yd (23cm)
ARTICHOKES
Pastel   GP07-P: ¼yd (23cm)
FORGET-ME-NOT ROSE
Stones   GP08-S: 1⅜yd (1.25m)
CHARD
Circus   GP09-C: ¼yd (23cm)

Backing fabric:

DAMASK
Stones   GP02-S: 3½yd (3.2m)

Binding:

PRESSED ROSES
02   PR 02: ½yd (45cm)

Batting:

61in x 85in (155cm by 216cm)

Quilting thread:

Grey machine quilting thread.

Templates:

See pages 89 & 90

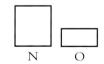

Kaffe's fascination with the way in which little pots are used decoratively in India inspired this quilt. The gentle colours of the shot cottons provide a perfect backdrop for the quirky little bottles.

PATCH SHAPES

The quilt centre is made of pieced blocks using two rectangular patches templates N & O. The top of each block is overlaid with an appliqué section and then each block has an appliqué bottle. The blocks are interspaced with sashing bars.

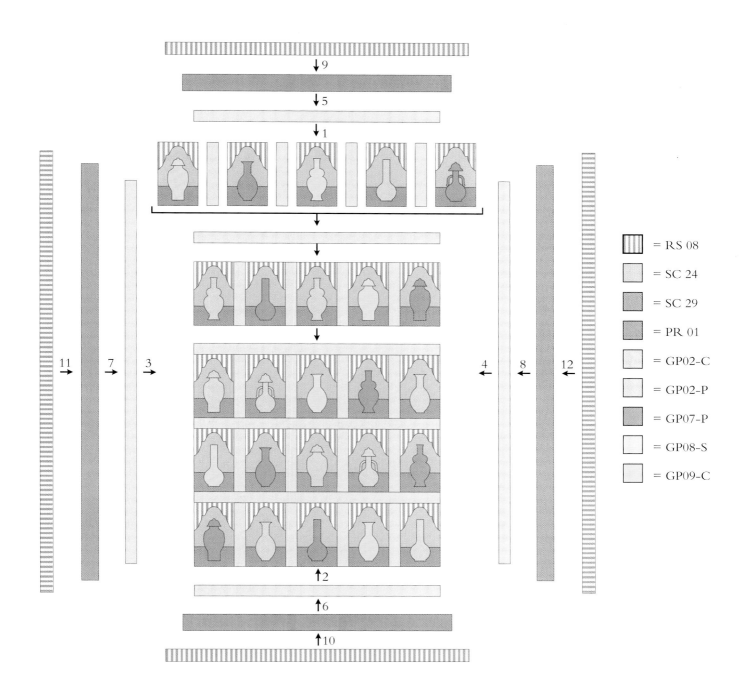

CUTTING OUT

Template N: Cut 8½in- (10cm-) wide strips across the width of the fabric. Each strip will give you 5 patches per 45in- (114cm-) wide fabric. Cut 25 in SC 24.
Template O: Cut 4in- (10cm-) wide strips across the width of the fabric.
Each strip will give you 11 patches per 45in- (114cm-) wide fabric. Cut 25 in SC 29.

Appliqué shapes (pages 87-89): remember to add a ¹⁄₄in seam allowance around appliqué templates.

Block overlay: Cut 5½in- (10cm-) wide strips across the width of the fabric. Each strip will give you 5 patches per 45in- (114cm-) wide fabric. Cut 25 in RS 08.
Bottle 1 (separate top): Cut 2 in GP09-C, 1 in PR 01, GP02-C, GP02-P, GP07-P.
Bottle 2: Cut 2 in GP09-C, 1 in PR 01, GP02-C, GP02-P, GP07-P.
Bottle 3: Cut 1 in PR 01, GP02-C, GP02-P, GP07-P, GP09-C.
Bottle 4: Cut 1 in PR 01, GP02-C, GP02-P, GP07-P, GP09-C.
Bottle 5 (separate top and handles): Cut 1 in GP02-C, GP02-P, GP07-P.

Sashing and inner borders: Cut 2½in- (6.5cm-) wide strips across the width of the fabric. Cut 4 strips 35¼in by 2½in (89.5cm x 6.5cm) for the inner side borders, 6 strips 43½in x 2½in (110.5cm x 6.5cm) 2 for the top and bottom inner borders and the remaining 4 for the horizontal sashing bars, 20 strips 12in by 2½in (30.5cm x 6.5cm) for the vertical sashing bars in GP08-S.

Middle Borders: Cut 3½in- (9cm-) wide strips across the width of the fabric. Cut 4 strips 38¼in x 3½in (97cm x 9cm) for the side middle borders. 4 strips 24in x 3½in (61cm x 9cm) for the top and bottom middle borders in PR 01.

Outer Borders: Cut 2¾in- (7cm-) wide strips across the width of the fabric. Cut 4 strips 40½in x 2¾in (103cm x 7cm) for the side outer borders. 4 strips 27in x 2¾in (68.5cm x 7cm) for the top and bottom outer borders in RS 08

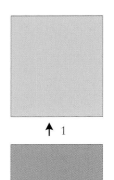

↑ 1

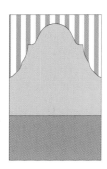

2

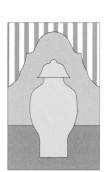

3

Straight cut binding: cut 7 strips 2¼in- (5.75cm-) wide from PR 02.
Backing: Cut 2 pieces, 61in x 43in (155cm by 110cm) in GP02-S.

MAKING THE BLOCKS

Using a ¼in (6mm) seam allowance throughout, make up 25 blocks using the block assembly diagrams as a guide. Add the striped overlay to each block, match the raw edges at the top carefully and then hand appliqué (see page 104) the lower edge to the background. Cut away the excess fabric behind the overlay leaving a ¼in (6mm) seam allowance. Hand appliqué a bottle to each block. The bottles should be placed 1½in (3.75cm) in from the bottom raw edge. For Bottle 1 layer the bottle top in front of the base. For Bottle 5 layer the handles behind the base and the bottle top in front of the base. Use the quilt assembly diagram as a guide.

ASSEMBLING THE ROWS

Assemble 5 rows of 5 blocks interspacing the blocks with short sashing bars, Interspace each row with a long sashing bar use the quilt assembly diagram as a guide to block placement.

MAKING THE BORDERS

Using a ¼in (6mm) seam allowance throughout join the top and bottom inner borders to the quilt centre. To make the side inner borders join 4 strips 35¼in by 2½in (89.5cm x 6.5cm) to make 2 strips 70in x 2½in (177.75cm x 6.5cm), join to the sides of the quilt centre.

To make the top and bottom middle borders join 4 strips 24in x 3½in (61 x 9cm) to make 2 strips 47½in x 3½in (120.5cm x 9cm). Join to the quilt centre. To make the side middle borders join 4 strips 38¼in x 3½in (97cm x 9cm) to make 2 strips 76in x 3½in (193 x 9cm). Join to the quilt centre.

To make the top and bottom outer borders join 4 strips 27in x 2¾in (68.5cm x 7cm) to make 2 strips 53½in x 2¾in (136cm x 7cm). Join to the quilt centre. To make the side outer borders join 4 strips 40½in x 2¾in (103cm x 7cm) to make 2 strips 80½in x 2¾in (204.5cm x 7cm). Join to the quilt centre.

FINISHING THE QUILT

Press the quilt top. Seam the backing pieces using a ¼in (6mm) seam allowance to form a piece 61in x 85in (155cm by 216cm) Layer the quilt top, batting and backing and baste together (see page 105). Using grey machine quilting thread quilt freeform swirling shapes in the star background areas. Quilt in the ditch along the seams lines, echo quilt the bottle outlines and the overlay shape as indicated in the quilting diagram. Quilt a large meander pattern in the middle and outer borders. Trim the quilt edges and attach the binding (see page 106).

Plaids Squared Quilt

★★

SALLY B. DAVIS

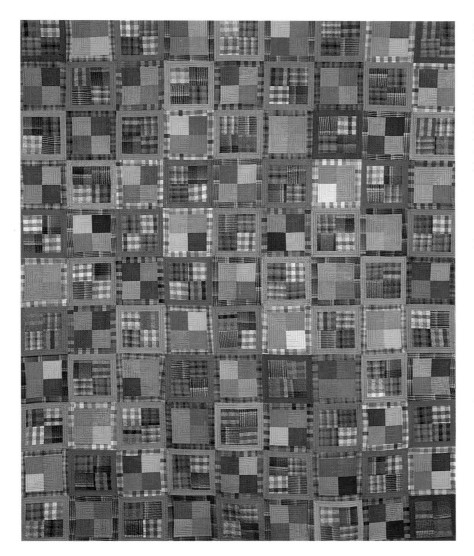

S ally has selected rich colours and a simple block design to create this wonderful quilt. Every possible combination of shot cotton and check fabric seems to have been used.

SIZE OF QUILT

The finished quilt will measure approx. 72in x 88in (183cm x 223cm).

MATERIALS

Patchwork Fabrics:

SHOT COTTON

Ginger	SC 01: ¼yd (23cm)
Cassis	SC 02: ¼yd (23cm)
Slate	SC 04: ⅛yd (15cm)
Opal	SC 05: ¼yd (23cm)
Thunder	SC 06: ¼yd (23cm)
Persimmon	SC 07: ⅛yd (15cm)
Raspberry	SC 08: ⅓yd (30cm)
Pomegranate	SC 09: ¼yd (23cm)
Bittersweet	SC 10: ¼yd (23cm)
Tangerine	SC 11: ¼yd (23cm)
Chartreuse	SC 12: ¼yd (23cm)
Navy	SC 13: ⅛yd (15cm)
Lavender	SC 14: ¼yd (23cm)
Denim	SC 15: ⅛yd (15cm)
Mustard	SC 16: ¼yd (23cm)
Sage	SC 17: ¼yd (23cm)
Tobacco	SC 18: ¼yd (23cm)
Lichen	SC 19: ¼yd (23cm)
Smoky	SC 20: ¼yd (23cm)
Pine	SC 21: ¼yd (23cm)
Pewter	SC 22: ⅛yd (15cm)
Stone Grey	SC 23: ⅛yd (15cm)
Ecru	SC 24: ⅛yd (15cm)
Grass	SC 27: ⅓yd (30cm)

EXOTIC CHECK

	EC 01: ⅓yd (30cm)
	EC 02: ⅓yd (30cm)
	EC 03: ¼yd (23cm)
	EC 05: ¼yd (23cm)

BROAD CHECK

	BC 01: ½yd (45cm)
	BC 02: ½yd (45cm)
	BC 03: ¼yd (23cm)
	BC 04: ½yd (45cm)

NARROW CHECK

	NC 01: ¼yd (23cm)
	NC 02: ⅓yd (30cm)
	NC 03: ⅓yd (30cm)
	NC 05: ¼yd (23cm)

Backing Fabric:

NARROW CHECK

NC 01: 5⅓yds (4.9m)

Bias binding:

PACHRANGI STRIPE

PS 15: ⅔yd (60cm)

Batting:

78in x 94in (198cm x 239cm).

Quilting thread:

Bright variegated machine quilting thread.

Templates:

See pages 91 & 92

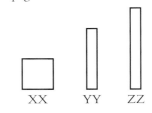

XX   YY   ZZ

PATCH SHAPES

The quilt is made up from pieced four patch blocks (template XX) each surrounded by a narrow border (templates YY and ZZ). The blocks are made in two colour combinations, shot cotton four patch centres with plaid narrow borders and plaid four patch centres with shot cotton narrow borders.

Quilt assembly

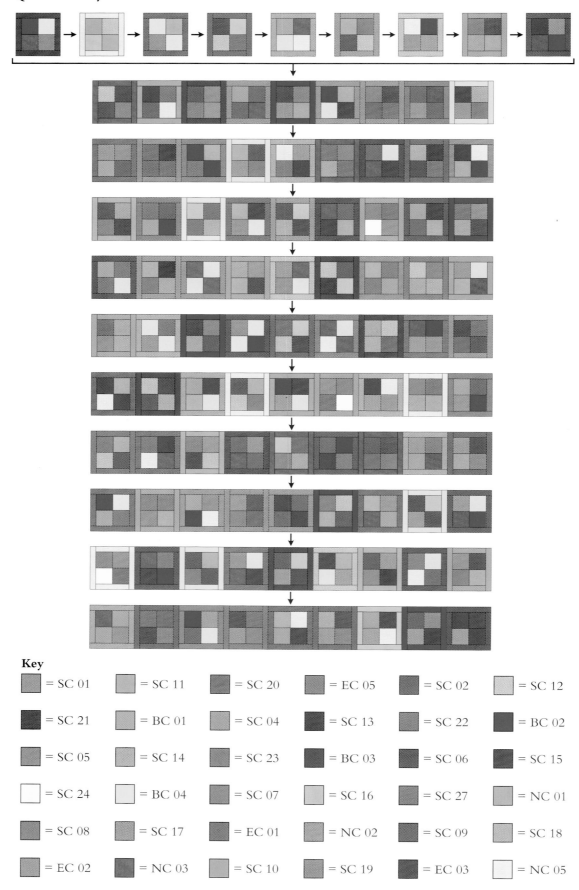

Key

= SC 01	= SC 11	= SC 20	= EC 05	= SC 02	= SC 12
= SC 21	= BC 01	= SC 04	= SC 13	= SC 22	= BC 02
= SC 05	= SC 14	= SC 23	= BC 03	= SC 06	= SC 15
= SC 24	= BC 04	= SC 07	= SC 16	= SC 27	= NC 01
= SC 08	= SC 17	= EC 01	= NC 02	= SC 09	= SC 18
= EC 02	= NC 03	= SC 10	= SC 19	= EC 03	= NC 05

CUTTING OUT

Template XX: Cut 3½in- (9cm-) wide strips across the width of the fabric. Each strip will give you 12 patches per 45in- (114cm-) wide fabric.

Cut 25 in BC 04, 22 in NC 03, 20 in NC 02, 18 in BC 02, EC 01, 17 in BC 01, SC 27, 16 in SC 08, 15 in EC 05, 14 in NC 01 and BC 03, 13 in NC 05, SC 06, SC 11, SC 12 and SC 14, 12 in EC 02, EC 03, SC 02, 11 in SC 21, 10 in SC 07, 9 in SC 16, 8 in SC 05, SC 09, SC 18 and SC 19, 7 in SC 01, SC 20, 5 in SC 13, SC 17, 3 in SC 04, SC 10, SC 15, SC 22 and SC 24, 1 in SC 23.

Template YY: Cut 1½in- (3.75cm-) wide strips across the width of the fabric. Each strip will give you 6 patches per 45in- (114cm-) wide fabric.

Cut 14 in BC 01, 12 in EC 01, 10 in BC 02, BC 04, SC 09, SC 27, 8 in BC 03, NC 02, NC 03, NC 05, SC 08, SC 14, SC 20, 6 in EC 02, EC 05, NC 01, SC 10, SC 12, SC 18, SC 21, 4 in SC 01, SC 02, SC 05, SC 06, SC 17, SC 19, 2 in EC 03, SC 04, SC 15, SC 16 and SC 22.

Template ZZ: Cut 1½in- (3.75cm-) wide strips across the width of the fabric. Each strip will give you 5 patches per 45in- (114cm-) wide fabric.

Cut 14 in BC 01, 12 in EC 01, 10 in BC 02, BC 04, SC 09, SC 27, 8 in BC 03, NC 02, NC 03, NC 05, SC 08, SC 14, SC 20, 6 in EC 02, EC 05, NC 01, SC 10, SC 12, SC 18, SC 21, 4 in SC 01, SC 02, SC 05, SC 06, SC 17, SC 19, 2 in EC 03, SC 04, SC 15, SC 16 and SC 22.

Block assembly

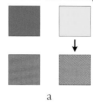

a

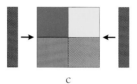

b

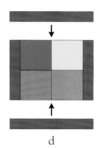

c

d

Bias binding: Cut 9½yds (8.7m) of bias binding 2in- (5cm-) wide from PS 15.

Backing: Cut 2 pieces 94in x 39in (238cm by 99cm).

MAKING THE BLOCKS

Using a ¼in (6mm) seam allowance throughout, make up 99 blocks, use the block assembly and quilt assembly diagrams as a guide.

MAKING UP THE ROWS

Assemble 11 rows of 9 blocks, use the quilt assembly diagram as a guide. Note: To reduce bulk on the seams, the blocks with plaid centres are all placed with the longer border strips horizontally and the blocks with shot cotton centres are turned so that the longer border strips are vertical.

FINISHING THE QUILT

Press the quilt top. Seam the backing pieces using a ¼in (6mm) seam allowance to form a piece 94in x 77½in (238cm by 197cm). Layer the quilt top, batting and backing and baste together (see page 105).

Using a bright variegated machine quilting thread, quilt a square spiral in the four patch section of the blocks with shot cotton centres (quilt fewer lines for a softer texture to the finished quilt) and a meander pattern in the four patch section of the blocks with plaid centres. Quilt two parallel lines in each block border, refer to the quilting diagram. Trim the quilt edges and attach the binding (see page 106).

Quilting diagram

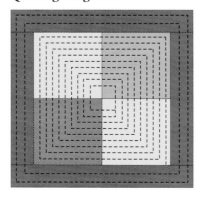

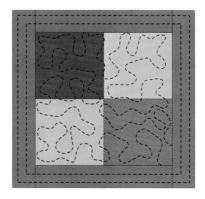

Melon Balls

LIZA PRIOR LUCY

★★★

Templates:
See page 90

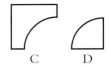

C   D

PATCH SHAPES
The whole quilt top is made from one block. Each block is made from one patch cut using template C and one cut using template D.

CUTTING OUT
Template C: Cut 224 in GP01-S for the centre section and 64 in RS 01 for the borders (RS 01 is reversible, so do not worry about the stripe direction at this stage).
Template D: Cut 58 in SC 35, 51 in SC 33, 48 in SC 34, 47 in SC 32, and 42 in SC 11 and SC 30.
Backing: Cut 1 piece 60in by 45in (152cm x 114cm) and 1 piece 60in x 22in (152cm x 56cm), use the remaining fabric for the bias binding, see below.
Bias Binding: Cut 7yds of (6.4m) of bias binding 2¼in- (6cm-) wide from RS 01.

MAKING THE PIECED BLOCKS
Using a ¼in (6mm) seam allowance follow the Curved seam piecing instructions (see page 103) to make up 288 pieced blocks using the key, block and quilt assembly diagrams as a guide for colour placement and stripe direction for the border blocks. Piece the centre blocks into groups of four and then into 8 rows of 7 groups. Piece the borders as indicated in the diagram and add in the order indicated.

FINISHING THE QUILT
Press the quilt top. Seam the two backing pieces together with a ¼in (6mm) seam allowance to form one piece approximately 60in x 66in (152cm x 168cm). Layer the quilt top, batting and backing and baste together (see page 105). Machine quilt using toning thread quilt as indicated on the quilting diagram. Trim the quilt edges and attach the bias binding (see page 106).

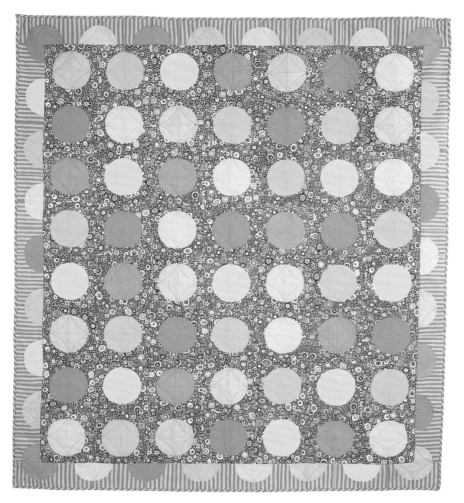

Sherbert coloured balls appear to hover over a printed carpet in this variation of the traditional pattern known as 'Drunkard's Path'. Liza has framed the quilt centre with a border of toning stripes and semi-circles.

SIZE OF QUILT
The finished quilt will measure approx. 63in x 56in (160cm x 142cm).

MATERIALS
Patchwork fabrics:
SHOT COTTON

Tangerine	SC 11: ½yd (45cm)
Custard	SC 30: ½yd (45cm)
Rosy	SC 32: ½yd (45cm)
Watermelon	SC 33: ½yd (45cm)
Lemon	SC 34: ½yd (45cm)
Sunshine	SC 35: ½yd (45cm)

ROMAN GLASS
Stones   GP01-S: 2¾yds (2.5 m)
ROWAN STRIPE
                    RS 01: ⅞yd (80cm)
Backing Fabric:
ROWAN STRIPE
                    RS 01: 3⅜yds (3.1m)
Bias Binding:
See backing fabric
Batting:
69in x 61in
Quilting thread:
Toning machine quilting thread.

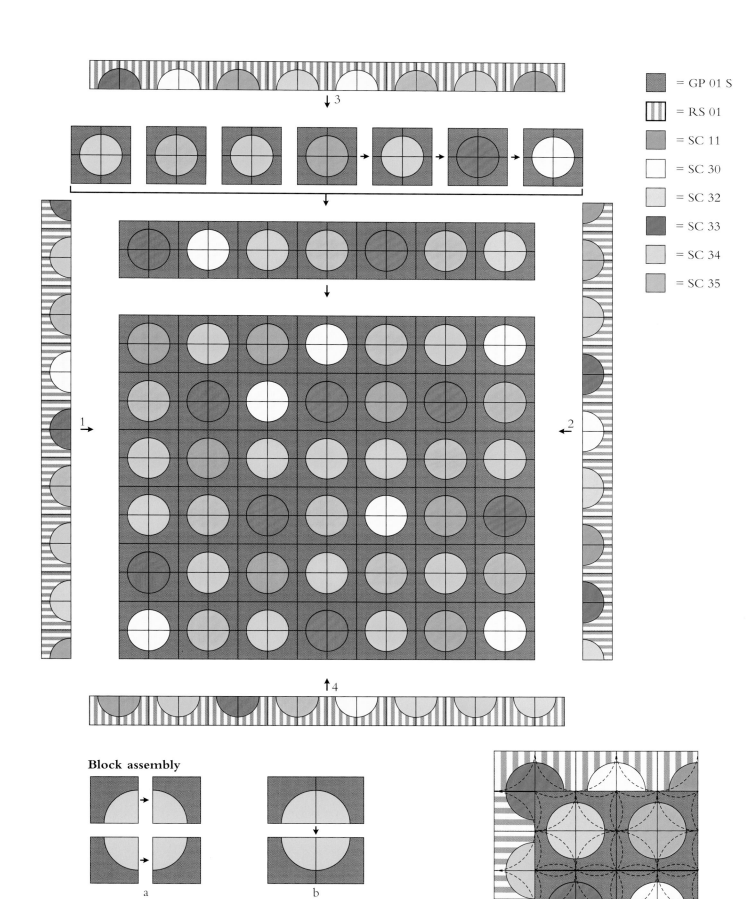

= GP 01 S

= RS 01

= SC 11

= SC 30

= SC 32

= SC 33

= SC 34

= SC 35

Block assembly

a

b

Marquetry Strip Baby Quilt

KAFFE FASSETT ★★

Ecru	SC 24: ⅛yd (15cm)
Putty	SC 29: ¼yd (23cm)
Watermelon	SC 33: ⅛yd (15cm)
Sunshine	SC 35: ⅛yd (15cm)

Backing fabric:
NARROW STRIPE

NS 17: 1½yds (1.35m)

Bias binding:
BROAD STRIPE

BS 01: ½yd (45cm)

Batting:
51in x 40in (130cm by 102cm)

Quilting thread:
Deep gold machine quilting thread.

Templates:
See pages 98–100

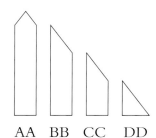

AA BB CC DD

EE FF GG HH II

JJ KK LL MM NN

OO PP QQ RR

Kaffe says "I was inspired by this stripe arrangement first as a carpet design".

SIZE OF QUILT

The finished quilt will measure approx. 47¾in x 35½in (121cm x 90cm).

MATERIALS

Patchwork fabrics:

SHOT COTTON

Slate	SC 04: ⅛yd (15cm)
Opal	SC 05: ¼yd (23cm)
Persimmon	SC 07: ⅛yd (15cm)
Raspberry	SC 08: ⅛yd (15cm)
Pomegranate	SC 09: ⅛yd (15cm)
Bittersweet	SC 10: ⅛yd (15cm)
Tangerine	SC 11: ⅛yd (15cm)
Lavender	SC 14: ⅛yd (15cm)
Mustard	SC 16: ½yd (45cm)
Lichen	SC 19: ¼yd (23cm)
Smoky	SC 20: ⅛yd (15cm)

Quilt assembly

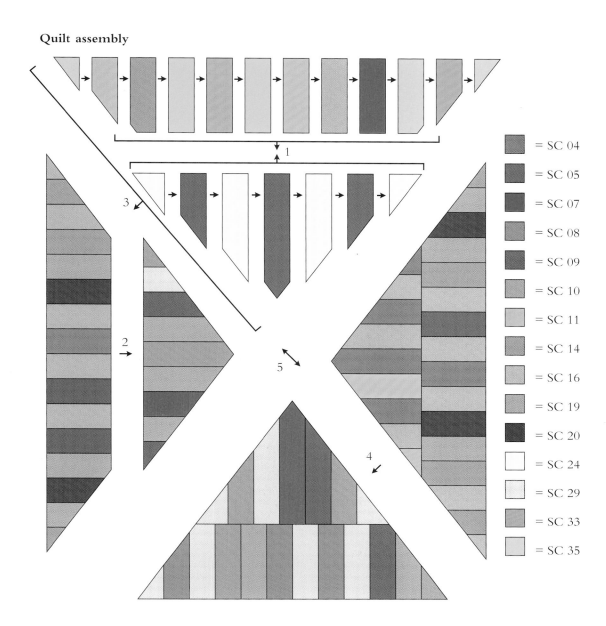

= SC 04
= SC 05
= SC 07
= SC 08
= SC 09
= SC 10
= SC 11
= SC 14
= SC 16
= SC 19
= SC 20
= SC 24
= SC 29
= SC 33
= SC 35

PATCH SHAPES

This quilt is made up of 18 different patch shapes cut from the templates illustrated here. Templates AA to DD are used for the inner top and bottom sections. Templates EE to II are used for the inner side sections. Templates JJ to NN are used for the outer side sections. Templates OO to RR are used for the outer top and bottom sections.

The templates for this quilt as printed at 50% of true size. Photocopy at 200% before using.

Note: You do not need to reverse the templates as Rowan Shot Cotton fabrics are fully reversible. If you are using non-reversible fabrics you will need to make additional reverse templates.

CUTTING OUT

Template AA: Cut 1 in SC 05, SC 07.
Template BB: Cut 2 in SC 24, 1 in SC 05, SC29.
Template CC: Cut 2 in SC 05, SC 10.
Template DD: Cut 2 in SC 24, SC 29.
Template EE: Cut 1 in SC 04, SC 10.

Template FF: Cut 2 in SC 19, 1 in SC11, SC16.
Template GG: Cut 2 in SC 04, 1 in SC 07, SC 09.
Template HH: Cut 2 in SC 16, 1 in SC 19, SC 29.
Template II: Cut 1 in SC 04, SC 09, SC 10, SC 11.
Template JJ: Cut 6 in SC 16, 3 in SC 05, 2 in SC 04, SC 19, SC 20, 1 in SC 14.
Template KK: Cut 2 in SC 14, SC 19.
Template LL: Cut 2 in SC 16, SC 20.
Template MM: Cut 2 in SC 14, SC 19.

Raindrops

BRANDON MABLY

★

Template NN: Cut 2 in SC 14, SC 16.
Template OO: Cut 2 in SC 08, SC 29
SC 35, 1 in SC 07, SC 10, SC 11, SC 16,
SC 19, SC 33.
Template PP: Cut 1 in SC 09, SC 10,
SC 29 SC 35.
Template QQ: Cut 1 in SC 08, SC 11,
SC 19, SC 33.
Template RR: Cut 2 in SC 35, 1 in
SC 10, SC 29.
Bias binding : cut 5yds of bias binding
2¹⁄₂in- (6.5cm-) wide from BS 01.
Backing: Cut 1 piece, 51in x 40in
(130cm by 102cm)

MAKING THE QUILT SECTIONS

Lay out all your cut patches in their
correct places according to the quilt
assembly diagram. Using a ¹⁄₄in (6mm)
seam allowance throughout, make up the
eight inner and outer quilt sections. Then
join the inner to the outer section in each
quarter section. Next join the top section
to the left side and the bottom to the
right side. Finally join the two halves
together at the diagonal centre seam.

FINISHING THE QUILT

Press the quilt top. Layer the quilt top,
batting and backing and baste together
(see page 105). Using deep gold machine
quilting thread quilt parallel wavy lines
in each colour area as shown in the
quilting diagram. Trim the quilt edges
and attach the binding (see page 106).

Quilting diagram

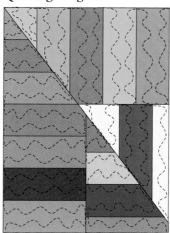

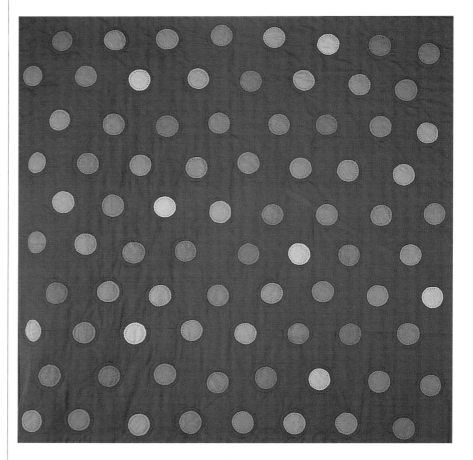

Brandon says of Raindrops "Working with the handsome
colour range of the shot cottons inspired me to create
something peaceful but strong, like raindrops breaking the water's
surface." Brandon has selected Slate, the perfect background
colour for the raindrops.

SIZE OF QUILT

The finished quilt will measure approx.
60in x 60in (152cm x 152cm).

MATERIALS

Background and binding fabric:
SHOT COTTON
Slate   SC 04: 3⁵⁄₈yds (3.3m)
Appliqué fabrics:
SHOT COTTON
Ginger   SC 01: ¹⁄₈yd (15cm)
Opal   SC 05: ¹⁄₈yd (15cm)
Raspberry   SC 08: ¹⁄₈yd (15cm)

Lavender   SC 14: ¹⁄₈yd (15cm)
Sage   SC 17: ¹⁄₄yd (23cm)
Tobacco   SC 18: ¹⁄₄yd (23cm)
Stone Grey   SC 23: ¹⁄₈yd (15cm)
Putty   SC 29: ¹⁄₈yd (15cm)
Mushroom   SC 31: ¹⁄₈yd (15cm)
Backing Fabric:
ROWAN STRIPE
                 RS05: 3⁵⁄₈yds (3.3m)
Batting:
65in x 65in
Quilting thread:
Toning hand quilting thread.

Quilt assembly

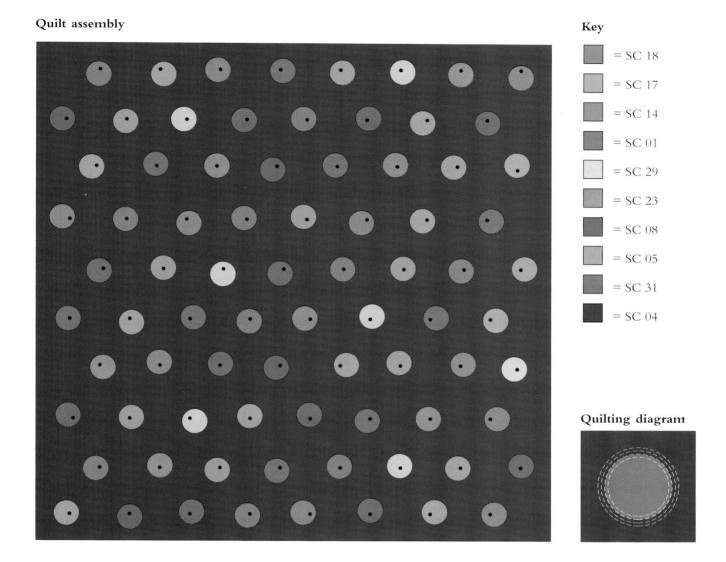

Key

▉	= SC 18
▉	= SC 17
▉	= SC 14
▉	= SC 01
▉	= SC 29
▉	= SC 23
▉	= SC 08
▉	= SC 05
▉	= SC 31
▉	= SC 04

Quilting diagram

Template:
See page 94

A

CUTTING OUT

Template A: Cut 13 in SC 18, 12 in SC 17, 10 in SC 05, 10 in SC 31, 8 in SC 01, 7 in SC 14, 7 in SC 23, 7 in SC 29, and 6 in SC 08.

Background: Cut 1 piece 65in by 45in (165cm x 114cm) and 1 piece 65in x 20in (165cm x 51cm).

Binding: Cut 4 strips 2½in x 65in (6.5cm x 165cm).

Backing: Cut 1 piece 65in x 45in (165cm x 114cm) and 1 piece 65in x 20in (165cm x 51cm).

MAKING AND MARKING THE BACKGROUND

Join the two fabric lengths to make a square approximately 64in x 64in (162cm x 162cm). Trim to 60½in x 60½in (154cm x 154cm).

The appliquéd circles are spaced on a grid. The rows are spaced at 7in (17.5cm) apart on the horizontal (total 8 rows) and 6in (15.25cm) apart on the vertical (total 10 rows) and are laid out as shown by the black dots on the diagram.

APPLIQUÉ

The appliqué circles are placed on the grid but each is slightly offset so the appearance is more random as shown in the diagram. Use the card template hand

appliqué method (see page 104). to prepare the circles and stitch into place.

FINISHING THE QUILT

Press the quilt top. Seam the two backing pieces together with a ¼in (6mm) seam allowance to form one piece approximately 64in x 64in (162cm x 162cm).

Layer the quilt top, batting and backing and baste together (see page 105).

Using the toning hand quilting thread, quilt four rows as indicated on the quilting diagram, they are spaced a ¼in intervals on and around each appliqué circle .

Trim the quilt edges and attach the binding (see page 106).

Smoky Stars

LIZA PRIOR LUCY

Templates:
See pages 95 & 96

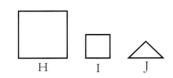

PATCH SHAPES

The quilt centre is made up of one large square, one small square and one triangle patch shape. These are pieced into sawtooth stars.

CUTTING OUT

Template H: Cut 5½in- (13.75cm-) wide strips across the width of the fabric. Each strip will give you 8 patches per 45in- (114cm-) wide fabric.
Cut 64 in GP15-G

Template I: Cut 3in- (7.75cm-) wide strips across the width of the fabric. Each strip will give you 14 patches per 45in- (114cm-) wide fabric.
Cut 128 in SC 17, SC 22

Template J: Cut 3½in- (8.75cm-) wide strips across the width of the fabric. Each strip will give you 24 patches per 45in- (114cm-) wide fabric.
Cut 256 in SC 17, SC 22, 72 in GP14-SG, SC 26, 64 in GP14-D, 56 in RS 06, RS 07, 40 in GP14-L, RS 05, SC 14, SC 36, 32 in GP07-P. Note: for the Rowan Stripe fabrics don't worry about the stripe directions as the fabrics are reversible.

Bias binding : cut 9⅓yds of bias binding 2½in- (6.5cm-) wide from RS 06.

Backing: Cut 2 pieces, 84in x 42½in (213cm by 108cm).

MAKING THE BLOCKS

Using a ¼in (6mm) seam allowance throughout, make up 64 blocks using the block and quilt assembly diagrams as a guide.

The subtle shading lends a new twist to this star quilt. See how Liza has cleverly placed the 'Bubbles' fabric in the centre of each star.

SIZE OF QUILT
The finished quilt will measure approx. 80in x 80in (203cm x 203cm).

MATERIALS
Patchwork fabrics:

SHOT COTTON
Lavender	SC 14:	¼yd (23cm)
Sage	SC 17:	2yds (1.8m)
Pewter	SC 22:	2yds (1.8m)
Duck Egg	SC 26:	⅓yd (30cm)
Lilac	SC 36:	¼yd (23cm)

ARTICHOKES
Pastel	GP07-P:	¼yd (23cm)

DOTTY
Lavender	GP14-L:	¼yd (23cm)
Sea Green	GP14-SG:	⅓yd (30cm)
Driftwood	GP14-D:	⅓yd (30cm)

BUBBLES
Grey	GP15-G:	1½yd (1.4m)

ROWAN STRIPE
	RS 05:	¼yd (23cm)
	RS 06:	⅓yd (30cm)
	RS 07:	⅓yd (30cm)

Backing fabric:
SHOT COTTON
Lichen	SC 19:	4¾yds (4.50m)

Bias Binding:
ROWAN STRIPE
	RS 06:	⅔yd (60cm)

Batting:
85in x 85in (216cm by 216cm)

Quilting thread:
Grey machine quilting thread.

Quilt assembly

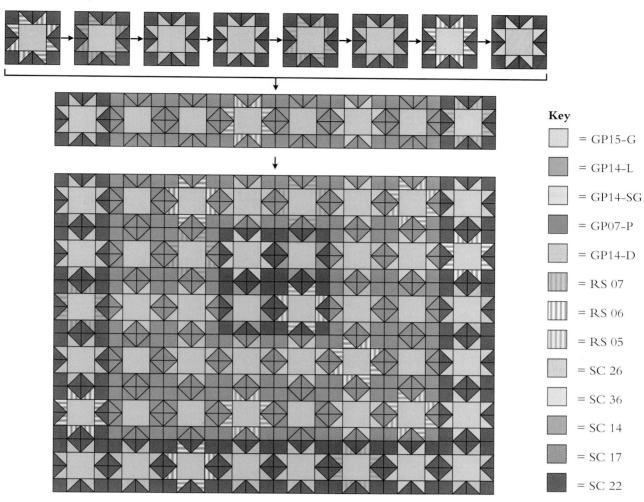

Key

= GP15-G

= GP14-L

= GP14-SG

= GP07-P

= GP14-D

= RS 07

= RS 06

= RS 05

= SC 26

= SC 36

= SC 14

= SC 17

= SC 22

Block assembly

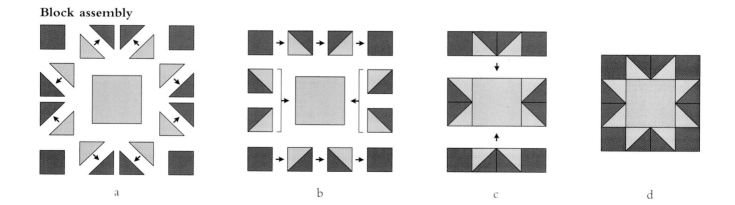

a   b   c   d

Twiggy Cushion

PAULINE SMITH ★

The star points are made in two colours, lavender and green. Keeping the two background fabrics separate, sort the green triangles from the lavender. There are 24 lavender stars, 4 on SC 22 background and 20 on SC 17 background. There are 40 green stars, 12 on SC 17 background and 28 on SC 22 background.

MAKING UP THE ROWS
Assemble 8 rows of 8 blocks, use the quilt assembly diagram as a guide to block placement.

FINISHING THE QUILT
Press the quilt top. Seam the backing pieces using a ¼in (6mm) seam allowance to form a piece 84in x 84in (213cm x 213cm) Layer the quilt top, batting and backing and baste together (see page 105). Using grey machine quilting thread quilt freeform swirling shapes in the star background areas. Quilt freeform bubble shapes on the grey star centres. Refer to the quilting diagram. Trim the quilt edges and attach the binding (see page 106).

Quilting diagram

A perfect project for those who have yet to try appliqué. The cushion top would also make a charming bag. Pauline dampened the appliqué shapes first as this made handling so easy.

SIZE OF CUSHION
The finished cushion will measure approx.16in x 17in (41cm x 44cm).

MATERIALS
Patchwork fabrics:
SHOT COTTON
Opal   SC 05: ½yd (45cm) cushion back included
Jade   SC 41: ½yd (45cm) cushion back included

Appliqué fabrics:
SHOT COTTON
Watermelon   SC 33: ⅛yd (15cm)
ROWAN STRIPE
                RS 07: ⅛yd (15cm)
ROMAN GLASS
Blue & White GP01-BW: ⅛yd (15cm)
Lining:
18in x 17in (46cm x 43cm)
Batting:
18in x 17in (46cm x 43cm)

Quilt assembly

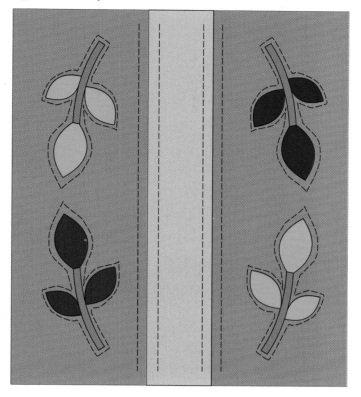

Key

= SC 05

= SC 41

= GP01–BW

= SC 33

= RS 07

Quilting thread:
Stranded cotton in peach, deep blue and lime green.

Templates:
See page 95

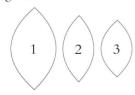

PATCH SHAPES

The cushion is made using rectangles of fabric cut at easily measured sizes, with appliquéd motifs.

CUTTING OUT

Cushion front:
Cut 2 pieces 6¾in x 18in (17cm x 46cm) in SC 41.

Cut 1 strip 3½in x 18in (9cm x 46cm) in SC 05.

Cushion back:
Cut 1 piece 16in x 10in (40.5cm x 25.5cm) in SC 41

Cut 1 piece 16in x 13in (40.5cm x 33cm) in SC05.

Appliqué shapes: Remember to add a ¼in seam allowance around all appliqué templates.
Cut 2 leaf shapes of each size in SC 33 and GP01-BW

Bias cut 4 stems 5in x ¾in (13cm x 2cm)

MAKING THE CUSHION FRONT

Using a ¼ in (6mm) seam allowance throughout, join the three front pieces with the narrow one in SC 05 in the middle.

APPLIQUÉ

Position the appliqué shapes as shown in the layout diagram. Hand appliqué the shapes into place tucking the base ends of the leaves under the stems (see hand appliqué on page 104)

QUILTING

Layer the cushion front, batting and lining and baste together (see page 105). Quilt ¼in (6mm) from the central seams on the SC 05 panel in peach, quilt ¼in (6mm) from the central seams on the SC 41 panels in deep blue and around each twig, ¼in (6mm) from the appliquéd shapes in lime green as indicated in the layout diagram.

FINISHING THE CUSHION

To finish the cushion follow the instruction on page 107.

Umbrella Quilt

KAFFE FASSETT

T his quilt was inspired by a patched umbrella made of old awning stripes seen in a Moroccan market. Blue prints and stripes alternate with the palest pink in this stunning quilt. Hand quilting in dark blue adds the finishing touch.

SIZE OF QUILT
The finished quilt will measure approx. 72in x 72in (183cm x 183cm).

MATERIALS
Patchwork Fabrics:
SHOT COTTON
Opal   SC 05: ¾yd (70cm)
Blush   SC 28: 2¾yds (2.50m)
ROMAN GLASS
Blue & White   GP01-BW: ½yd (45cm)
ARTICHOKES
Circus   GP07-C: 1¼yds (1.15m)

PRESSED ROSES
    PR 03: ¾yd (70cm)
    PR 07: 1yd (90cm)
Backing Fabric:
BLUE & WHITE STRIPE
    BWS02: 4¼yds (3.90m)
Binding Fabric:
PRESSED ROSES
    PR 03: ½yd (45cm)
Batting:
76in x 76in (193cm x 193cm).
Quilting thread:
Dark blue perlé cotton thread.

Template:
See page 96

CCC

PATCH SHAPES
The quilt centre is made up from large triangular sections which are foundation pieced. The borders are made up from one square patch shape (template CCC) pieced into a checkerboard pattern.

CUTTING OUT
Borders (cut these first and reserve the remaining fabrics for the foundation piecing): Cut 3½in- (9cm-) wide strips across the width of the fabric. Each strip will give you 12 patches per 45in- (114cm-) wide fabric.
Cut 88 in SC 26, 23 in GP07-C, 22 in GP01-BW & PR 07, 21 in PR 03.
Strips for foundation piecing:
(Cut strips across the width of the fabric as you need them for the foundation piecing)
From fabric SC 28 cut 2½in strips
From fabric SC 05 cut 2½in strips
From fabric GP01-BW cut 2in strips
From fabric GP07-C cut 4in and 2in strips
From fabric PR 03 cut 4in strips
From fabric PS 07 cut 4in strips
Binding: Cut 7 strips 2in- (5cm-) wide x width of fabric in PR 03.
Backing: Cut 1 piece 76in x 45in (193cm by 114cm) and 1 piece 76in x 32in, (193cm by 81cm) in BWS 02.

FOUNDATION PIECING
Make up the 16 sections using the foundation piecing method on page 103. When you have completed the foundation sections join as shown in the quilt assembly diagram. Do not remove the papers yet!

MAKING THE PIECED BORDERS
Stitch the fabric patches into pairs always pressing towards the printed fabric. Stitch the pairs into sections using the quilt layout diagram as a guide to fabric placement. Join the borders to the quilt centre in the order indicated.

Quilt assembly

FINISHING THE QUILT

Remove the foundation papers. Press the quilt top. Seam the backing pieces using a ¼in (6mm) seam allowance to form a piece 76in x 76in (193cm by 193cm). Layer the quilt top, batting and backing and baste together (see page 105). Using dark blue perlé cotton thread, quilt by hand with large bold stitches as indicated in the quilting diagram. Trim the quilt edges and attach the binding (see page 106).

Quilting diagram

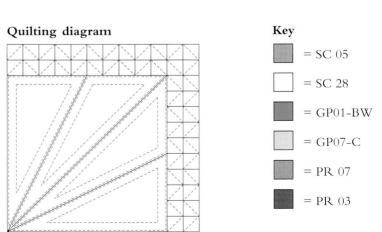

Key

	= SC 05
	= SC 28
	= GP01–BW
	= GP07–C
	= PR 07
	= PR 03

Birds In The Air

ROBERTA HORTON

★★

Lemon	SC 34: $\frac{1}{8}$yd (15cm)
Sunshine	SC 35: $\frac{1}{8}$yd (15cm)
Lilac	SC 36: $\frac{1}{8}$yd (15cm)
Lime	SC 43: $\frac{1}{8}$yd (15cm)
ROMAN GLASS	
Circus	GP01-C: $\frac{1}{8}$yd (15cm)
Gold	GP01-G: $\frac{1}{8}$yd (15cm)
Leafy	GP01-L: $\frac{1}{8}$yd (15cm)
Pastel	GP01-P: $\frac{1}{8}$yd (15cm)
Pink	GP01-PK: $\frac{1}{8}$yd (15cm)
Red	GP01-R: $\frac{1}{4}$yd (23cm)
Stones	GP01-S: $\frac{1}{8}$yd (15cm)
GAZANIA	
Circus	GP03-C: $\frac{1}{4}$yd (23cm)
Pastel	GP03-P: $\frac{1}{4}$yd (23cm)
FORGET ME NOT ROSE	
Circus	GP08-C: $\frac{1}{4}$yd (23cm)
Leafy	GP08-L: $\frac{1}{4}$yd (23cm)
Stone	GP08-S: $\frac{1}{4}$yd (23cm)
CHARD	
Jewel	GP09-J: $\frac{1}{4}$yd (23cm)
FLORAL DANCE	
Magenta	GP12-MG: $\frac{1}{4}$yd (23cm)
Ochre	GP12-O: $\frac{1}{4}$yd (23cm)
Pink	GP12-P: $\frac{1}{4}$yd (23cm)
CHRYSANTHEMUM	
Green	GP13-GN: $\frac{1}{4}$yd (23cm)
Red	GP13-R: $\frac{1}{4}$yd (23cm)
Ochre	GP13-O: $\frac{1}{4}$yd (23cm)
DOTTY	
Driftwood	GP14-D: $\frac{1}{8}$yd (15cm)
Lavender	GP14-L: $\frac{1}{8}$yd (15cm)
Ochre	GP14-O: $\frac{1}{8}$yd (15cm)
Plum	GP14-P: $\frac{1}{8}$yd (15cm)
Sea Green	GP14-SG: $\frac{1}{8}$yd (15cm)
BUBBLES	
Grey	GP15-G: $\frac{1}{8}$yd (15cm)
Ochre	GP15-O: $\frac{1}{8}$yd (15cm)
Sky Blue	GP15-S: $\frac{1}{8}$yd (15cm)
ROWAN STRIPE	
	RS 01: $\frac{1}{8}$yd (15cm)
	RS 02: $\frac{1}{8}$yd (15cm)
	RS 05: $\frac{1}{8}$yd (15cm)
	RS 07: $\frac{1}{8}$yd (15cm)

Roberta has cleverly arranged pastel and jewel colours in a selection of prints, shot cottons and stripes to make this lively quilt. The plaid border is the perfect finishing touch.

We have included a full fabric listing as usual, however you could use up scraps from other Rowan projects.

Border Fabric:
BROAD CHECK
01 – BC 01: $1\frac{1}{2}$yds (1.35m)
Backing Fabric:
NARROW STRIPE
17 – NS 17: $2\frac{1}{4}$yds (2.05m)

SIZE OF QUILT
The finished quilt will measure approx. 48 in x 60 in (122cm x 152cm).

MATERIALS
Patchwork Fabrics:
DAMASK
| Citrus | GP02-CT: $\frac{1}{4}$yd (23cm) |
| Jewel | GP02-J: $\frac{1}{4}$yd (23cm) |

SHOT COTTON
Chartreuse	SC 12: $\frac{1}{8}$yd (15cm)
Lavender	SC 14: $\frac{1}{8}$yd (15cm)
Lichen	SC 19: $\frac{1}{8}$yd (15cm)
Ecru	SC 24: $\frac{1}{8}$yd (15cm)
Duck Egg	SC 26: $\frac{1}{8}$yd (15cm)
Grass	SC 27: $\frac{1}{8}$yd (15cm)
Rosy	SC 32: $\frac{1}{8}$yd (15cm)
Watermelon	SC 33: $\frac{1}{8}$yd (15cm)

Quilt assembly

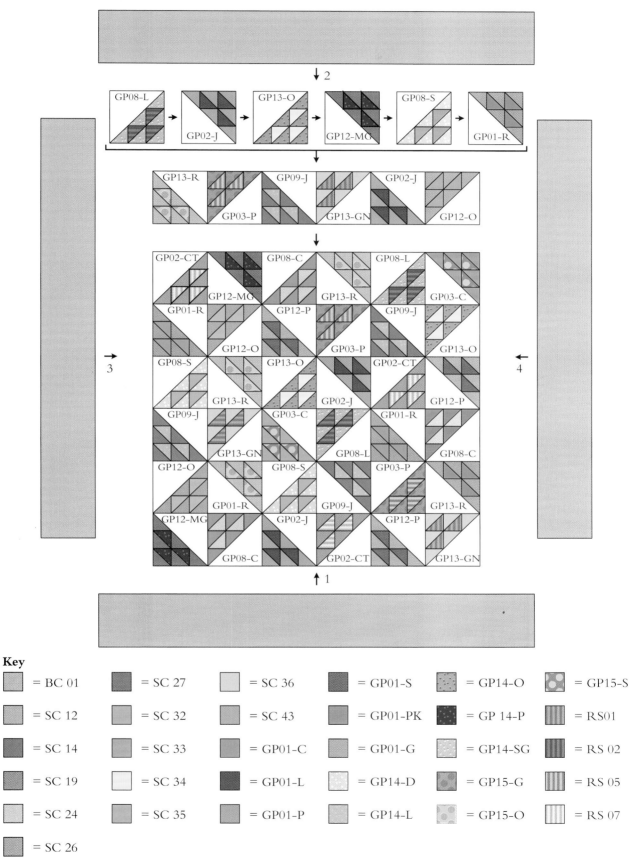

Binding Fabric:
NARROW CHECK
03 - NC 03: ½yd (45cm)
Batting:
52in x 64in (132cm x 163cm).
Quilting thread:
Dark cream quilting thread.

Templates:
See page 94

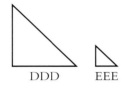

PATCH SHAPES
The quilt centre is made up from blocks of two triangular patches (templates DDD and EEE).

CUTTING OUT
Template DDD: Cut 7in- (17.75cm-) wide strips across the width of the fabric. Cut 4 in GP01-R, GP02-J, GP09-J, GP13-R, 3 in GP02-CT, GP03-P, GP08-C, GP08-L GP08-S, GP12-MG, GP12-O, GP12-P, GP13-GN, GP13-O, 2 in GP03-C.

Template EEE: Cut 3in- (7.75cm-) wide strips across the width of the fabric. Each strip will give you 24patches per 45in- (114cm-) wide fabric.
Cut 24 in SC 12, SC 14, SC 19, SC 43, 18 in SC 26, SC 27, SC 36, GP01-G, GP01-P, GP01-PK, GP14-D, GP14-O, GP14-SG, GP15-G, 12 in SC 33, GP01-C, GP01-L, GP14-L, GP15-O, 9 in SC 24, SC 32, SC 34, SC 35, GP01-S, GP14-P, RS 01, RS 02, RS 05, RS 07, 6 in GP15-S.

Borders: from the length of the fabric cut 4 strips 6½in x 48½ (16.5cm x 123) in BS 01.

Binding: cut 6 strips 2in- (5cm-) wide x width of fabric in NC 03.

Backing: Cut 1 piece 52in by 45in (132cm x 114cm) and 2 pieces 26¼in x 20in, (67cm by 51cm).

Block assembly

a

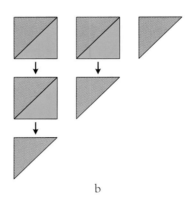

b

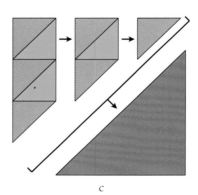

c

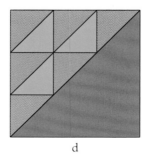

d

MAKING THE BLOCKS
Using a ¼ in (6mm) seam allowance throughout, make up 48 blocks using the block assembly diagrams as a guide along with the quilt assembly diagram for fabric placement.

MAKING UP THE ROWS
Assemble 8 rows of 6 blocks, use the quilt assembly diagram as a guide.

MAKING THE BORDERS
Join the borders to the quilt centre in the order indicated on the quilt assembly diagram.

FINISHING THE QUILT
Press the quilt top. Using a ¼in (6mm) seam allowance, seam the 2 smaller backing pieces to make a piece 52in by 19½in (132cm x 49.5cm) then seam this piece to the large backing piece to form a piece 64in x 52in (132cm x 163cm). Layer the quilt top, batting and backing and baste together (see page 105). Using the deep cream toning thread, machine quilt in a large meander design. Roberta highlighted some of the flower motifs on the printed fabrics and quilted a geometric pattern following the lines in the fabric on the borders. (see page 106 for more information on machine quilting). Trim the quilt edges and attach the binding (see page 106).

Nursery Teatime

★★★

ROSE VERNEY

The unusual collection of motifs in subtle, earthy colours Rose has appliquéd onto this play rug will surely spark the imagination of any child. You may prefer to use the rug as a bed cover or to decorate the nursery wall. Take your favourite motif and make a matching laundry bag or cushion.

SIZE OF QUILT

The finished quilt will measure approx. 60in x 61¼ in (152cm x 156cm).

MATERIALS

Patchwork and Appliqué Fabrics:

SHOT COTTON

Sage	SC 17: ¼yd (23cm)
Lichen	SC 19: ¼yd (23cm)
Pine	SC 21: ½yd (45cm)
Pewter	SC 22: ½yd (45cm)
Stone Grey	SC 23: ⅔yd (70cm)
Ecru	SC 24: 1yd (90cm)
Charcoal	SC 25: ¾yd (70cm)
Duck Egg	SC 26: 1yd (90cm)
Grass	SC 27: ¾yd (70cm)
Custard	SC 30: ⅛yd (15cm)
Apple	SC 39: ½yd (45cm)
Cobalt	SC 40: ¼yd (23cm)

Backing Fabric:

SHOT COTTON

Stone Grey SC23: 2¾yds (2.50m)

Binding Fabric:

SHOT COTTON

Grass SC 27: see patchwork fabrics.

Cobalt SC 40: see patchwork fabrics.

Batting:

64in x 64in (162cm x 162cm).

Quilting thread:

Soft white crochet cotton.

PATCH SHAPES

The quilt centre is made up five 12in wide rows of rectangles cut to specific sizes.

CUTTING OUT

Cut 12½in- (31.75cm-) wide strips across the width of the fabric. All rectangles are 12½ in- (31.75cm-) wide and are quoted from the top to bottom of each row as shown in the layout diagram. Note: leave the selvedges on some rectangles.

Row 1:

SC 23: 8in (20.5cm)
SC 25: 5¼in (13.25cm)
SC 21: 3¼in (8.25cm)
SC 25: 4¾in (12cm)
SC 23: 7¼in (18.5cm)
SC 22: 8¾in (22.25cm)
SC 23: 8½in (21.5cm)
SC 21: 3in (7.5cm)
SC 25: 7½in (19cm)
SC 21: 1½in (3.75cm)
SC 23: 7¾in (19.75cm)
SC 21: 1¾in (4.5cm)

Row 2:

SC 24: 2¼in (5.75cm)
SC 39: 8in (20.25cm)
SC 26: 9½in (24cm)
SC 24: 4in (10.25cm)
SC 26: 4¾in (12cm)
SC 26: 4½in (11.5cm)
SC 24: 6¾in (17.25cm)
SC 39: 4¼in (10.75cm)
SC 24: 7¾in (19.75cm)
SC 26: 3¾in (9.5cm)
SC 39: 1¾in (4.5cm)
SC 24: 10in (25.25cm)

Row 3:

SC 25: 7¼in (18.50cm)
SC 23: 6¾in (17.25cm)
SC 22: 7½in (19.00cm)
SC 25: 4in (10.25cm)

Quilt assembly

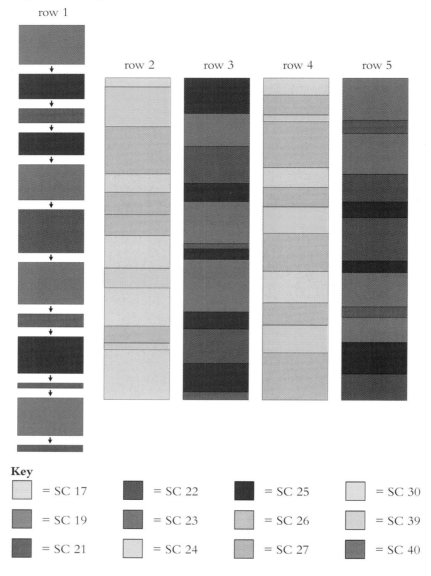

row 1

row 2

row 3

row 4

row 5

Key

■ = SC 17	■ = SC 22	■ = SC 25	■ = SC 30
■ = SC 19	■ = SC 23	■ = SC 26	■ = SC 39
■ = SC 21	■ = SC 24	■ = SC 27	■ = SC 40

SC 23: 8½in (21.50cm)
SC 21: 1½in (3.75cm)
SC 25: 2½in (6.25cm)
SC 23: 10½in (26.75cm)
SC 25: 3¾in (9.5cm)
SC 22: 7in (17.75cm)
SC 25: 6in (15.25cm)
SC 21: 2in (5cm)
Row 4:
SC 24: 3¾in (9.5cm)
SC 26: 4¼in (10.75cm)
SC 39: 1¾in (4.5cm)
SC 26: 9¼in (23.5cm)
SC 24: 4¼in (10.75cm)
SC 26: 4¼in (10.75cm)
SC 39: 5½in (14cm)
SC 26: 7¾in (19.75cm)

SC 24: 6½in (16.5cm)
SC 26: 4¾in (12cm)
SC 39: 5¾in (14.5cm)
SC 26: 9½in (24.25cm)
Row 5:
SC 23: 8½in (21.50cm)
SC 21: 3in (7.5cm)
SC 23: 8¼in (21cm)
SC 22: 5¾in (14.5cm)
SC 25: 3½in (9cm)
SC 22: 8¾in (22.25cm)
SC 25: 2¾in (7cm)
SC 23: 7in (17.75cm)
SC 21: 2½in (6.25cm)
SC 23: 5¼in (13.5cm)
SC 25: 6½in (16.5cm)
SC 22: 5½in (14cm)

Appliqué shapes (pages 83-85): remember to add a ¼in seam allowance around all appliqué templates.

Cut appliqué shapes using the templates on pages 83, 84 and 85 using the quilt appliqué diagram as a guide to colours and quantities. Some shapes are reversed for variety.

Binding: cut 6 strips 2¾in- (7cm-) wide x width of fabric in SC 27 and 2 pieces 7 in x 2¾in (18cm x 7cm) in SC 40.
Backing: Cut 1 piece 64in x 44in (162cm by 114cm) and 2 pieces 32¼in x 20½in, (82cm by 52cm).

Quilt Appliqué Diagram

Key

= SC 17	= SC 22	= SC 25	= SC 30
= SC 19	= SC 23	= SC 26	= SC 39
= SC 21	= SC 24	= SC 27	= SC 40

MAKING UP THE ROWS

Assemble 5 rows in the order listed in the cutting instruction, use the quilt assembly diagram as a guide. Note: Rose comments that she likes the texture of the fabric selvedges and has used them to give texture the quilt. Instead of joining rectangles in the usual way, where the fabric has a selvedge along one edge overlap it on top of the next piece and topstitch it in place using a ¼in (6mm) seam allowance and leaving the edge free.

WORKING THE APPLIQUÉ

Place the appliqué shapes onto the pieced rows as shown in the quilt appliqué diagram and hand appliqué in place (see page 104)

JOINING THE ROWS

Join the rows in the order indicated in the quilt appliqué diagram.

FINISHING THE QUILT

Press the quilt top. Using a ¼in (6mm) seam allowance, seam the 2 smaller backing pieces to make a piece 64in by 20½in (162cm x 52cm) then seam this piece to the large backing piece to form a piece 64in x 64in (162cm x 162cm).

Layer the quilt top, batting and backing and baste together (see page 105). Using soft cream crochet cotton, work large running stitches all over the quilt. Use the stitching to add details to the appliqué shapes such as a feather in the hat, whiskers and a tail on the cat, steam rising from a tea cup and decoration on the teapot. The stitching is not only decorative, it acts as quilting to secure the layers together. Trim the quilt edges and attach the binding, using the small sections of SC 40 along the top right and bottom left edges of the quilt. (see page 106).

Chrysanthemum Soft Squares

KAFFE FASSETT

DOTTY
Driftwood   GP14-D: 1½yds (1.35m)
Lavender   GP14-L: 1yd (90cm)
Sea green   GP14-SG: ¼yd (23cm)
Terracotta   GP14-T: ⅓yd (30cm)
Backing Fabric:
CHRYSANTHEMUM
Grey   GP13-GR: 5¼yds (4.80m)★
Binding Fabric:
CHRYSANTHEMUM
Grey   GP13-GR: ⅔yd (60cm)★
★GP13-GR total for whole project,
8½yds (7.70m)
Batting:
81in x 92in (205cm x 234cm).
Quilting thread:
Toning machine quilting thread.

Templates:
See pages 93 & 94

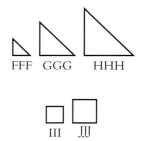

PATCH SHAPES

The quilt centre is made up from one triangle (template GGG) pieced into square blocks, interspaced with large setting squares (no template, cut to size) and setting triangles (template HHH). You'll find half template HHH on page 94. Take a large piece of paper, fold, place edge of template HHH to fold of paper, trace around shape and cut out. Open out for the complete template. Triangles (template GGG) are used in the four corners of the quilt centre. The quilt has an inner border with a square at each corner (template III). The middle border is pieced from two blocks, the four patch' from one square (template III) and the square in a square' made from one square and one triangle (templates JJJ and FFF). The outer border repeats the inner border with a square at each corner (template III).

Kaffe wanted a light, almost opal–like look as though delicate washes of colour have been overlaid to give a gently faded texture to this quilt. This was made easy by flipping some of the fabrics to the wrong side, a useful technique for giving a vintage look to new fabrics.

SIZE OF QUILT
The finished quilt will measure approx.
77 in x 88 in (195cm x 223cm).

MATERIALS
Patchwork and Border Fabrics:
ROMAN GLASS
Pastel   GP01-P: ¼yd (23cm)
FORGET-ME-NOT-ROSE
Circus   GP08-C: ¼yd (23cm)
Leafy   GP08-L: ¼yd (23cm)
Stone   GP08-S: ¼yd (23cm)

DAMASK
Circus   GP02-C: ¼yd (23cm)
Citrus   GP02-CT: ¼yd (23cm)
Leafy   GP02-L: ¼yd (23cm)
Pastel   GP02-P: ¼yd (23cm)
Stone   GP02-S: ¼yd (23cm)
ARTICHOKES
Pastel   GP07-P: ¾yd (70cm)
CHARD
Pastel   GP09-P: ¼yd (235cm)
CHRYSANTHEMUM
Grey   GP13-GR: 2½yd (2.30m)★

Block assembly

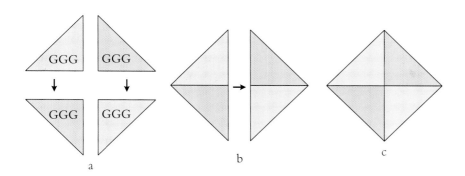

a

b

c

Four patch border corner block

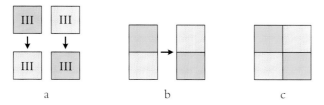

a

b

c

Square in a square border block

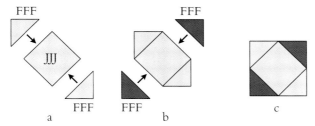

a

b

c

CUTTING OUT

Note: some fabrics are used wrong side facing in some positions for a softer look. Check the fabric key for more information.

Template FFF (middle borders): Cut 3⅝in- (9.25cm-) wide strips across the width of the fabric. Each strip will give you 24 patches per 45in- (114cm-) wide fabric.

Cut 96 in GP07-P(WS) and GP14-D.

Template GGG: Cut 6⅜in- (16.25cm-) wide strips across the width of the fabric. Each strip will give you 12 patches per 45in- (114cm-) wide fabric.

Cut 8 in GP01-P, GP02-L(WS), GP02-C(WS), GP02-CT,(WS), GP02-P(WS), GP02-S, GP07-P(WS), GP08-C, GP08-L, GP08-S, GP09-P(WS), GP14-D(WS), GP14-L(WS), GP14-SG(WS), GP14-T(WS), 4 in GP13-GR (use the off-cuts from cutting template HHH below for these 4 triangles).

Template HHH: Cut 12⅜in (31.5cm) squares, cut diagonally in both directions, this will avoid bias edges along the sides of the quilt when piecing. Each square will give 4 patches.

Cut 20 in GP13-GR.

Template III (borders): Cut 3¼in- (8.25cm-) wide strips across the width of the fabric. Each strip will give you 13 patches per 45in- (114cm-) wide fabric.

Cut 16 in GP14-T(one patch is used right side facing), 8 in GP14-SG(WS).

Template JJJ (middle borders): Cut 4⅜in- (11.25cm-) wide strips across the width of the fabric. Each strip will give you 10 patches per 45in- (114cm-) wide fabric.

Cut 48 in GP13-GR.

Setting Squares: Cut 20 squares 8¼in x 8¼in for setting in GP13-GR.

Inner and Outer Borders: For side inner borders cut 4 strips 33½in x 3¼in (85cm x 8.25cm) and for top and bottom inner borders cut 4 strips 28in x 3¼in (71cm x 8.25cm) in GP15-L(WS). For side outer borders cut 4 strips 41¾in x 3¼in (106cm x 8.25cm) and for top and bottom inner borders cut 4 strips 36¼in x 3¼in (92cm x 8.25cm) in GP15-L(WS).

Binding: cut 8 strips 2½in- (6.5cm-) wide x width of fabric in GP13-GR.

Backing: Cut 2 pieces 92in x 41in (234cm by 104cm).

MAKING THE QUILT CENTRE

Using a ¼ in (6mm) seam allowance throughout, make up 30 blocks, use the quilt and block assembly diagrams as a guide. Arrange the blocks with the setting squares and triangles (template HHH) into 10 diagonal rows following the quilt assembly diagram. Join the blocks into rows, then join the rows together to form the quilt centre. Join one smaller triangle (template GGG) to each corner to complete the quilt centre.

MAKING THE INNER BORDERS

Join the side inner border strips to form 2 strips 66½ in x 3¼in (169cm x 8.25cm). Join the top and bottom inner border strips to form 2 strips 55½in x 3¼in (141cm x 8.25cm) Join one square (template III) to each end of the top and bottom borders. Join the borders to the quilt centre in the order indicated by the quilt assembly diagram.

Quilt assembly

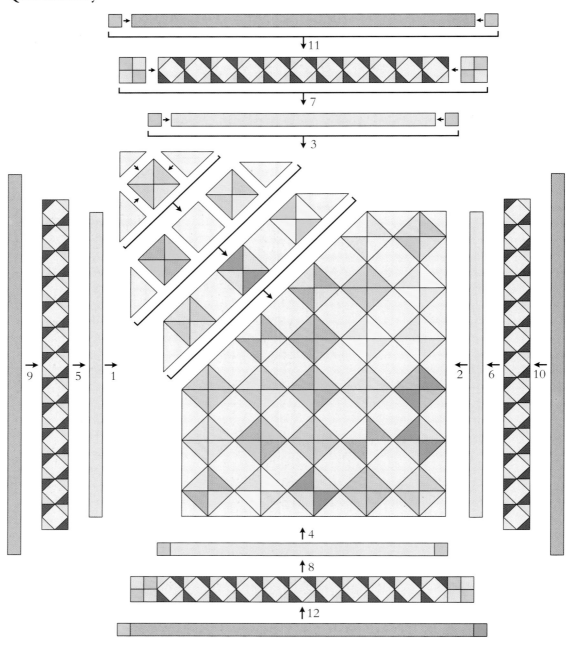

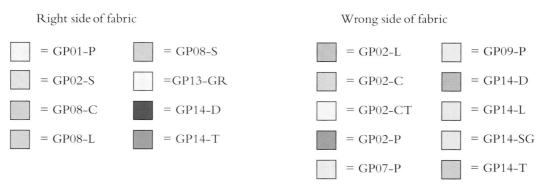

Key

Right side of fabric

= GP01-P		= GP08-S	
= GP02-S		=GP13-GR	
= GP08-C		= GP14-D	
= GP08-L		= GP14-T	

Wrong side of fabric

= GP02-L		= GP09-P	
= GP02-C		= GP14-D	
= GP02-CT		= GP14-L	
= GP02-P		= GP14-SG	
= GP07-P		= GP14-T	

Salsa Bag
KIM HARGREAVES

MAKING THE MIDDLE BORDERS

Make up 48 'square in a square' blocks using the block assembly guide. Join the blocks into 2 rows with 13 blocks for the side middle borders and 2 rows with 11 blocks for the top and bottom middle borders. Make up 4 'four patch' corner blocks following the block assembly guide, join one to each end of the top and bottom borders. Join borders to the quilt centre in the order indicated by the quilt assembly diagram.

MAKING THE OUTER BORDERS

Join the side outer border strips to form 2 strips 83 in x 3¼in (211cm x 8.25cm). Join the top and bottom outer border strips to form 2 strips 72in x 3¼in (183cm x 8.25cm) Join one square (template III) to each end of the top and bottom borders. Join the borders to the quilt centre in the order indicated by the quilt assembly diagram.

FINISHING THE QUILT

Press the quilt top. Seam the backing pieces using a ¼in (6mm) seam allowance to form a piece 92in x 81in (234cm by 205cm). Layer the quilt top, batting and backing and baste together (see page 105). Using a toning thread, machine quilt in large meandering floral pattern. (See page 106 for more information on machine quilting). Trim the quilt edges and attach the binding (see page 106).

With vibrant colours and simple appliqué Kim has designed this elegant shoulder bag which will just tuck under the arm

SIZE OF BAG

The finished bag will measure approx. 11½ in x 10 in (29cm x 26cm).

MATERIALS

Fabrics:
SHOT COTTON
Cassis   SC 02: ½yd (45cm)

Persimmon	SC 07:	⅛yd (15cm)
Pomegranate	SC 09:	⅛yd (15cm)
Bittersweet	SC 10:	⅛yd (15cm)
Tangerine	SC 11:	⅛yd (15cm)
Watermelon	SC 33:	½yd (45cm)

Finishing materials:
½ yd medium weight iron on interfacing
1½yd piping cord ¼in- (6mm) thick

Templates:
See page 87

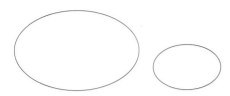

APPLIQUÉ SHAPES

The bag is appliquéd with two sizes of oval, the smaller layered on the larger.

CUTTING OUT

Bag front and back:
Cut 2 pieces 12¾in x 10¾in (32.5cm x 27cm) in SC 33.

Lining:
Cut 2 pieces 2in x 10¾in (5cm x 27cm) in SC 33.
Cut 2 pieces 10¾in x 10¾in (27cm x 27cm) in SC 02.

Interfacing:
Cut 2 pieces 12¾in x 10¾in (32.5cm x 27cm).

Handles:
Bias cut 2 strips 1¼in x 22in (3cm x 56cm) in SC 02.

Appliqué shapes: Remember to add a ¼in seam allowance around all appliqué templates.

Cut 16 large ovals in SC 02
Cut 6 small ovals in SC 10, 5 in SC 07, 3 in SC 11 and 2 in SC 09,

APPLIQUÉ

Form the oval shapes using the card templates method (see page 104) Position one small oval on each of the large ovals and stitch into place. Position the large ovals on the bag front as indicated in the diagram. Baste and stitch into place. (see hand appliqué on page 104)

FINISHING THE BAG

Note: Use a ⅜in seam allowance throughout and stitch with right sides together unless otherwise stated.

1. Press interfacing to the wrong side of bag front and back. Stitch the bag front

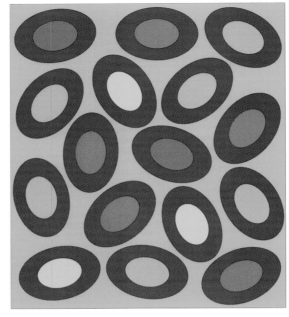

= SC 02
= SC 07
= SC 09
= SC 10
= SC 11
= SC 33

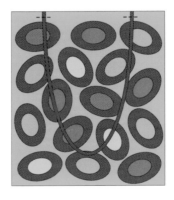

and back together along the side and bottom edges, turn to right side.

To make the lining sew one 10¾in x 2in (5cm x 27.5cm) strip of SC 33 to each of the 10¾in x10¾in SC 02 pieces. Press. Match the lining pieces right sides together with the SC 33 strips at the top. Stitch the side seams and turn to right side.

2. To make the handles cut two 22in (56cm) lengths of piping cord. Take the two bias strips 1¼in x 22in (3cm x 56cm), fold each one in half and stitch using a ⅜ in seam allowance to make a casing for the piping cord. Trim the seam allowance, turn to the right side. Bind the end of the piping cords tightly with

sticky tape, sew through the end of the cord using a large blunt needle and strong thread. Thread the needle through the casing pulling the piping cord through carefully, it will be very tight.

3. Position the handles onto the right side of the bag front and back with the raw edges level with the bag top and 2¼in in from the side seams, sew securely into place. Turn the bag inside out and place the lining inside the bag so the lining and bag are right sides together and the strips in SC 33 are at the top of the bag.

Sew around the top of the bag, turn through and carefully press the top edge. Hem the bottom edge of the lining.

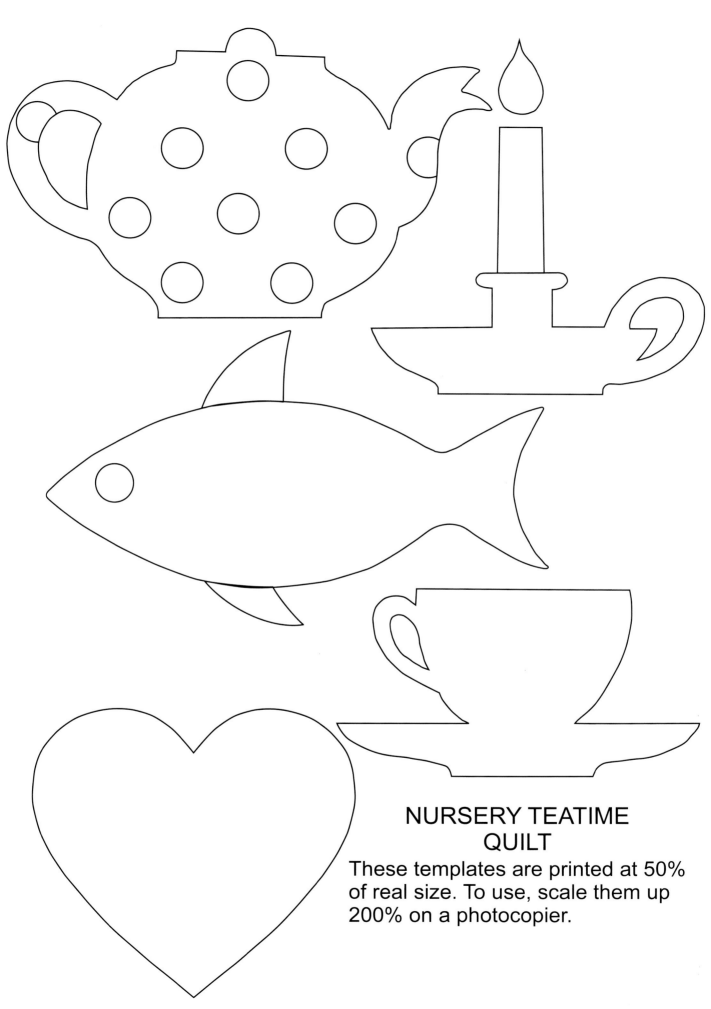

NURSERY TEATIME
QUILT

These templates are printed at 50% of real size. To use, scale them up 200% on a photocopier.

NURSERY TEATIME
QUILT

These templates are printed at 50% of real size. To use, scale them up 200% on a photocopier.

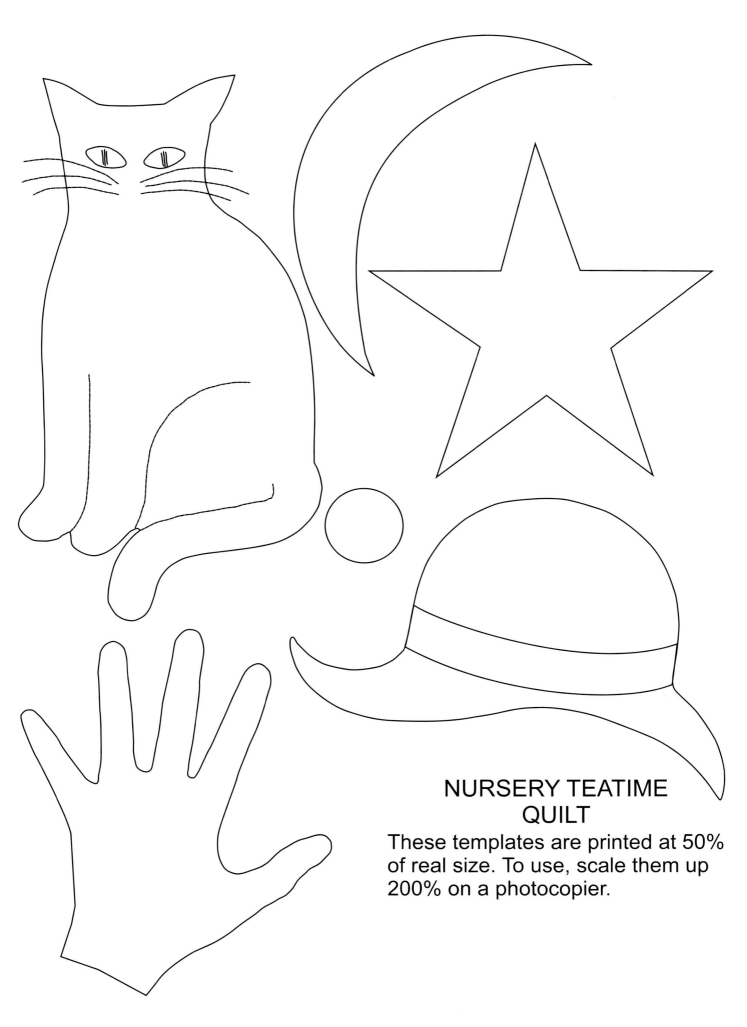

NURSERY TEATIME QUILT

These templates are printed at 50% of real size. To use, scale them up 200% on a photocopier.

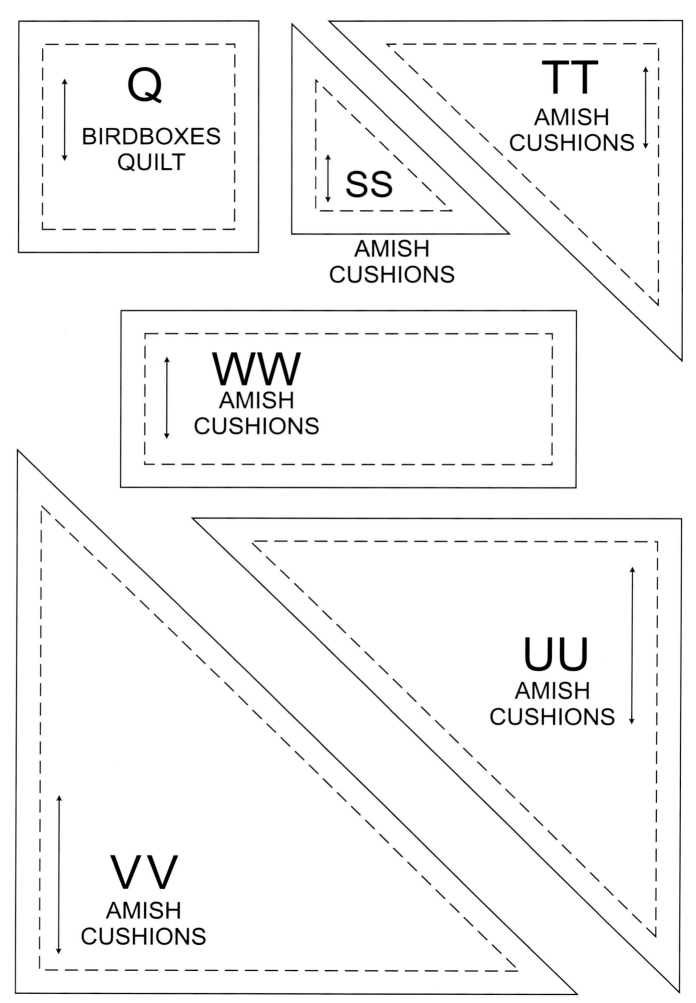

Q
BIRDBOXES
QUILT

SS
AMISH
CUSHIONS

TT
AMISH
CUSHIONS

WW
AMISH
CUSHIONS

UU
AMISH
CUSHIONS

VV
AMISH
CUSHIONS

SALSA BAG

SALSA BAG

1

LITTLE BOTTLES
QUILT

2

LITTLE BOTTLES
QUILT

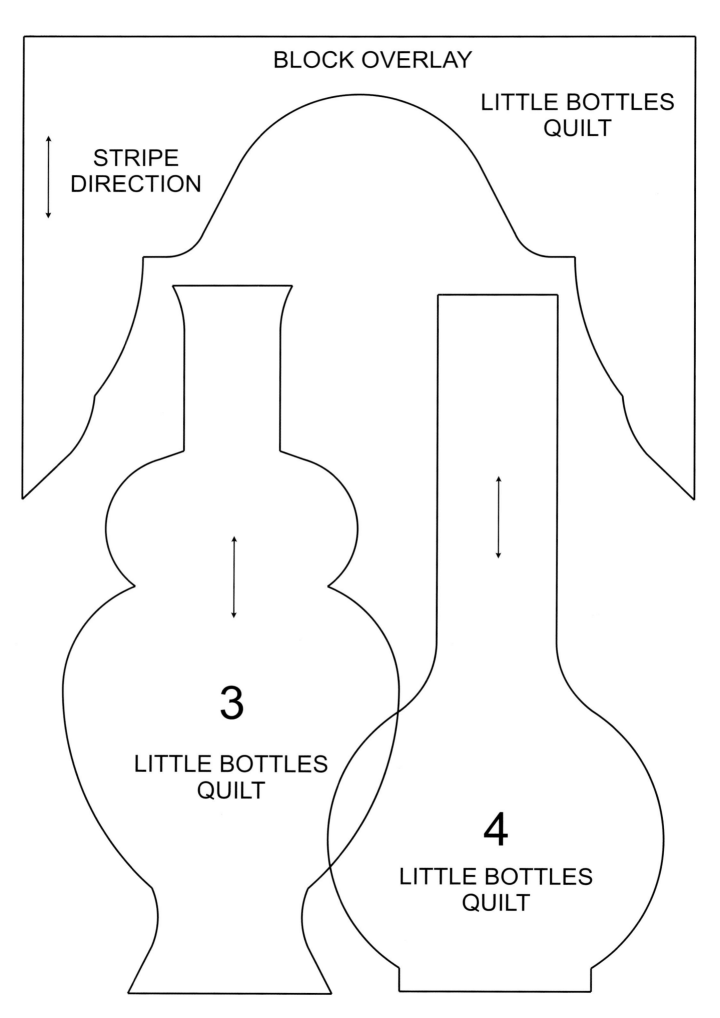

BLOCK OVERLAY

LITTLE BOTTLES
QUILT

STRIPE
DIRECTION

3

LITTLE BOTTLES
QUILT

4

LITTLE BOTTLES
QUILT

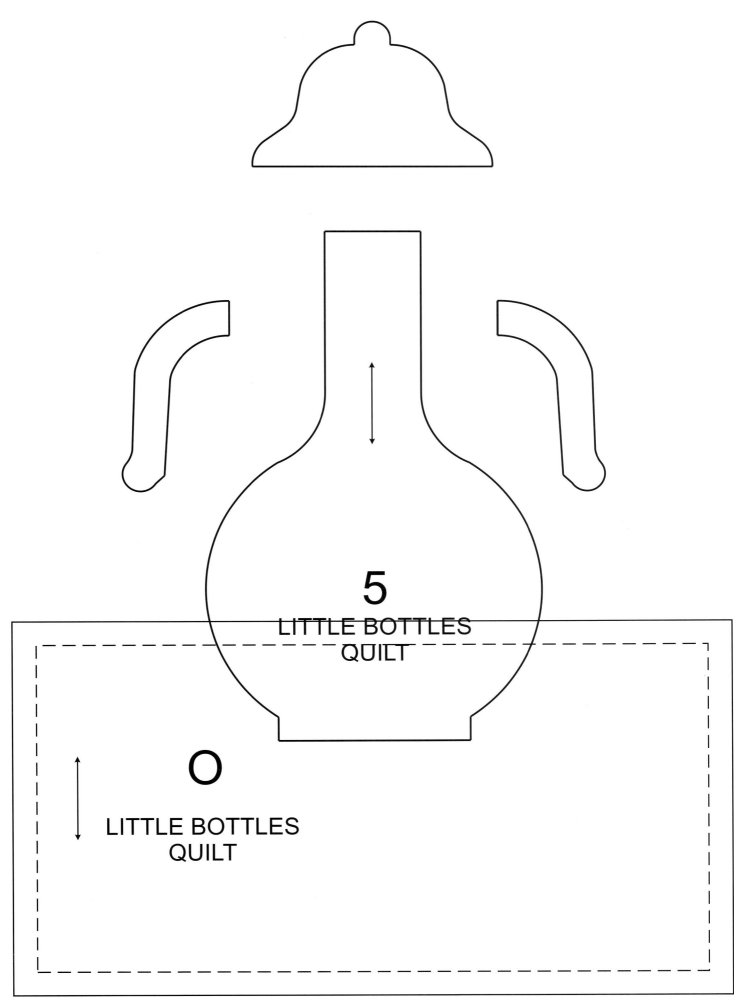

5
LITTLE BOTTLES
QUILT

O
LITTLE BOTTLES
QUILT

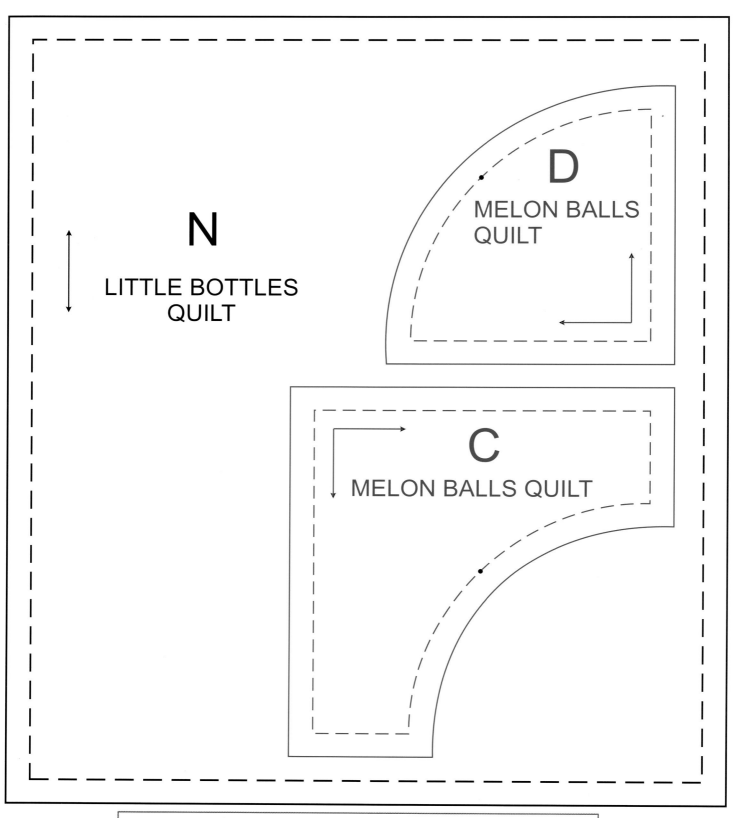

N

LITTLE BOTTLES
QUILT

D

MELON BALLS
QUILT

C

MELON BALLS QUILT

K

HUNDREDS AND THOUSANDS QUILT

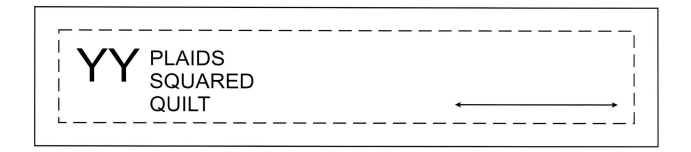

YY PLAIDS SQUARED QUILT

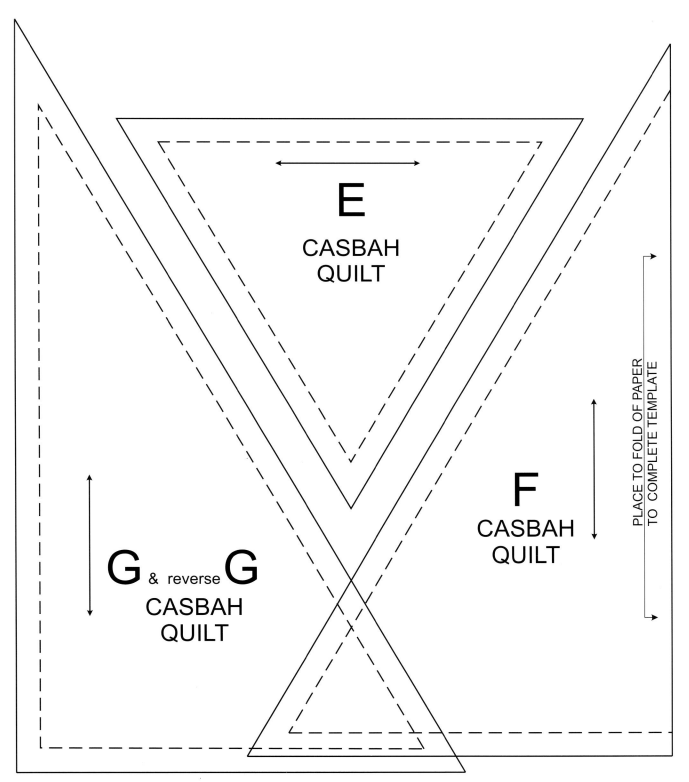

E CASBAH QUILT

F CASBAH QUILT

G & reverse **G** CASBAH QUILT

PLACE TO FOLD OF PAPER TO COMPLETE TEMPLATE

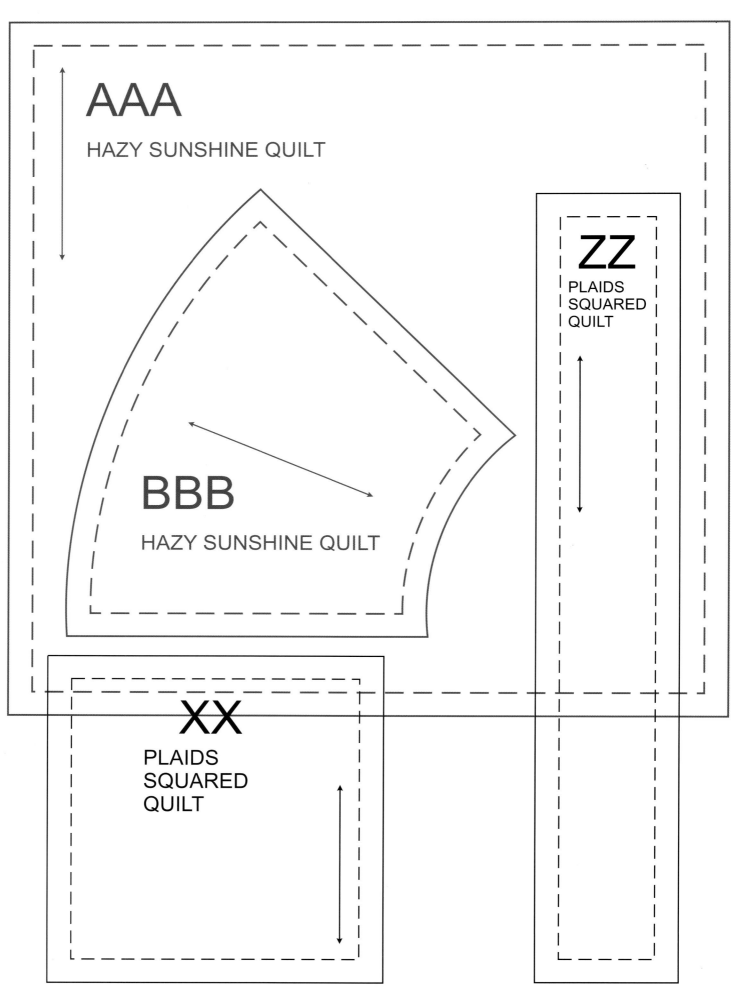

AAA

HAZY SUNSHINE QUILT

ZZ

PLAIDS
SQUARED
QUILT

BBB

HAZY SUNSHINE QUILT

XX

PLAIDS
SQUARED
QUILT

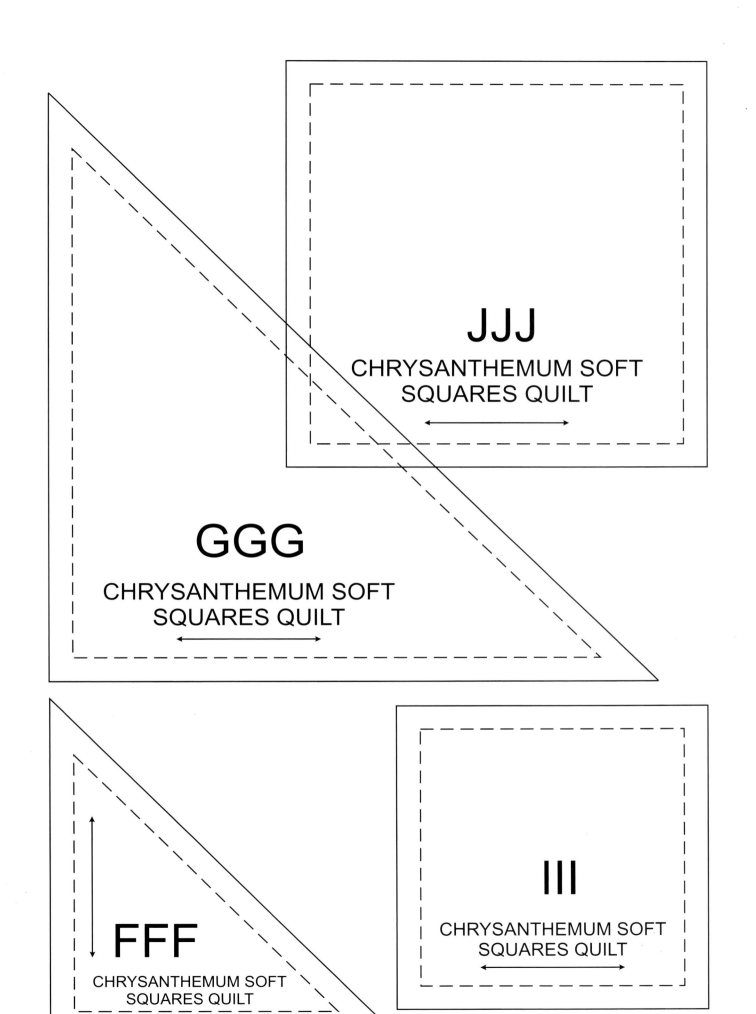

JJJ

CHRYSANTHEMUM SOFT
SQUARES QUILT

GGG

CHRYSANTHEMUM SOFT
SQUARES QUILT

FFF

CHRYSANTHEMUM SOFT
SQUARES QUILT

III

CHRYSANTHEMUM SOFT
SQUARES QUILT

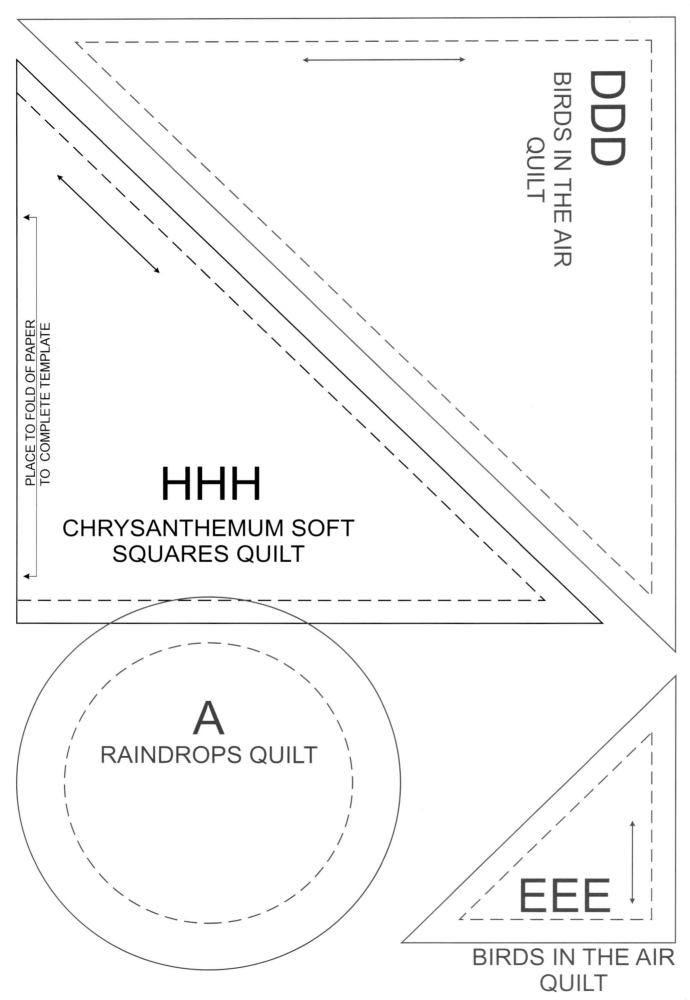

DDD
BIRDS IN THE AIR
QUILT

PLACE TO FOLD OF PAPER
TO COMPLETE TEMPLATE

HHH
CHRYSANTHEMUM SOFT
SQUARES QUILT

A
RAINDROPS QUILT

EEE

BIRDS IN THE AIR
QUILT

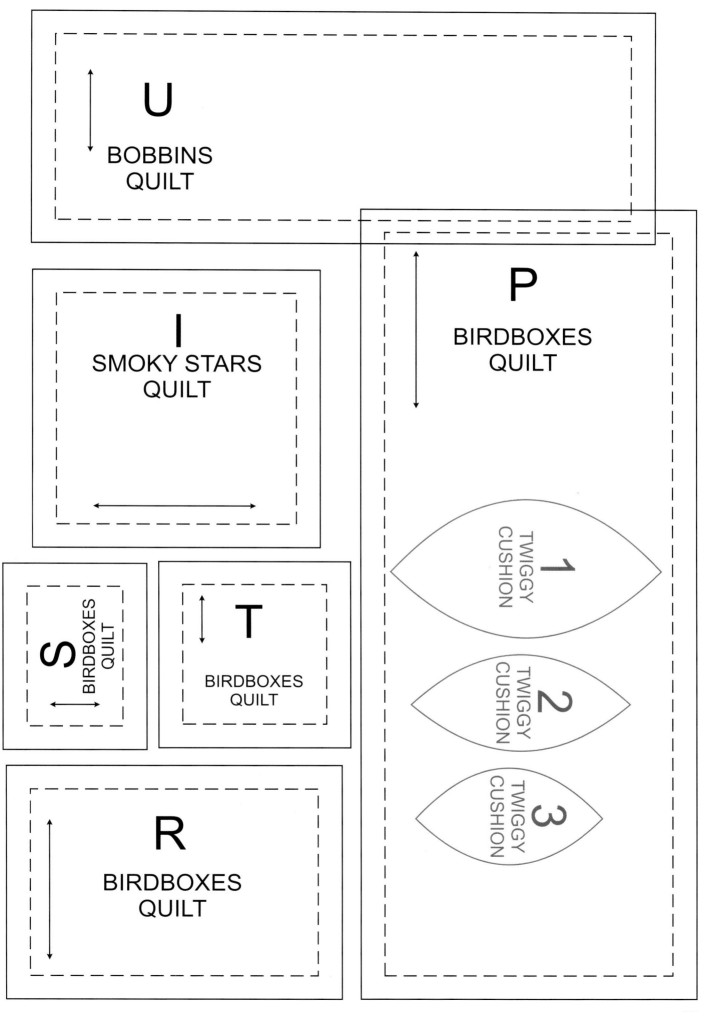

U
BOBBINS
QUILT

I
SMOKY STARS
QUILT

P
BIRDBOXES
QUILT

S
BIRDBOXES
QUILT

T
BIRDBOXES
QUILT

R
BIRDBOXES
QUILT

1
TWIGGY
CUSHION

2
TWIGGY
CUSHION

3
TWIGGY
CUSHION

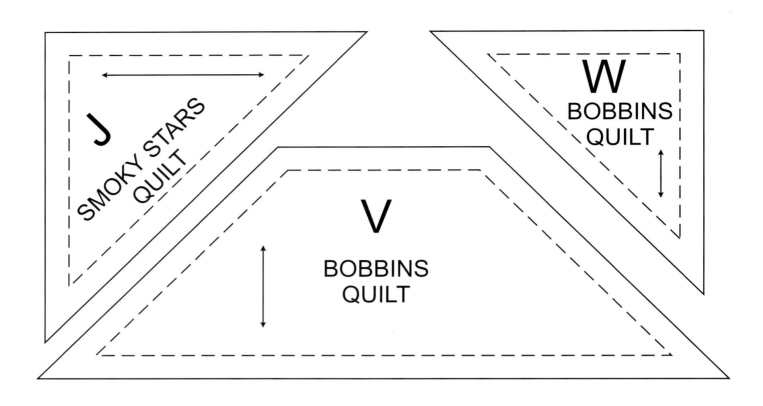

J
SMOKY STARS
QUILT

W
BOBBINS
QUILT

V
BOBBINS
QUILT

H

SMOKY STARS
QUILT

CCC

UMBRELLA QUILT

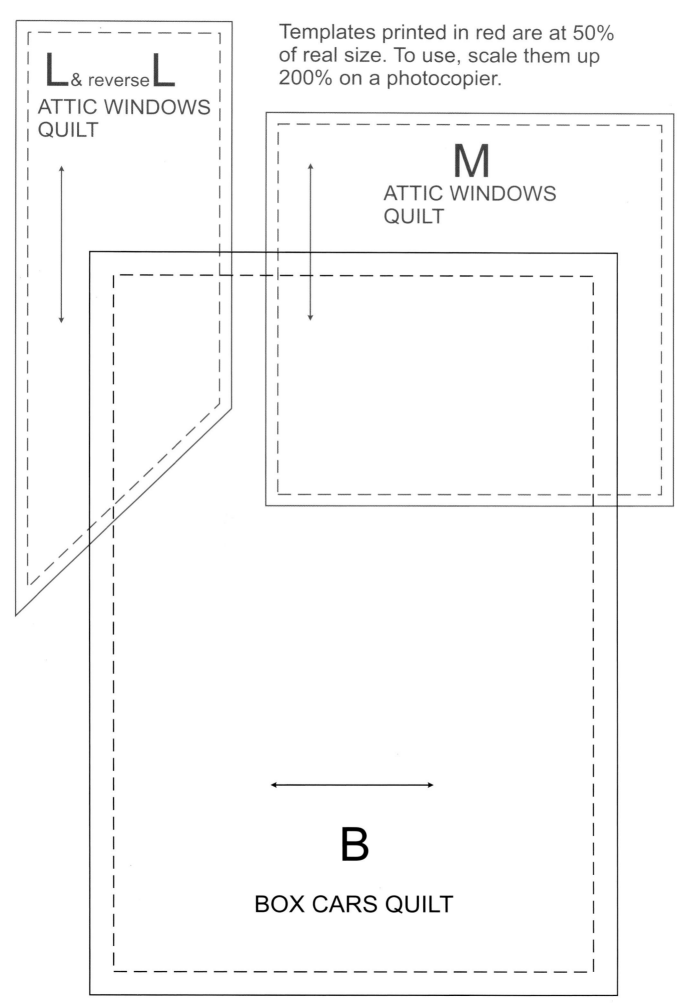

L & reverse L
ATTIC WINDOWS
QUILT

Templates printed in red are at 50%
of real size. To use, scale them up
200% on a photocopier.

M
ATTIC WINDOWS
QUILT

B

BOX CARS QUILT

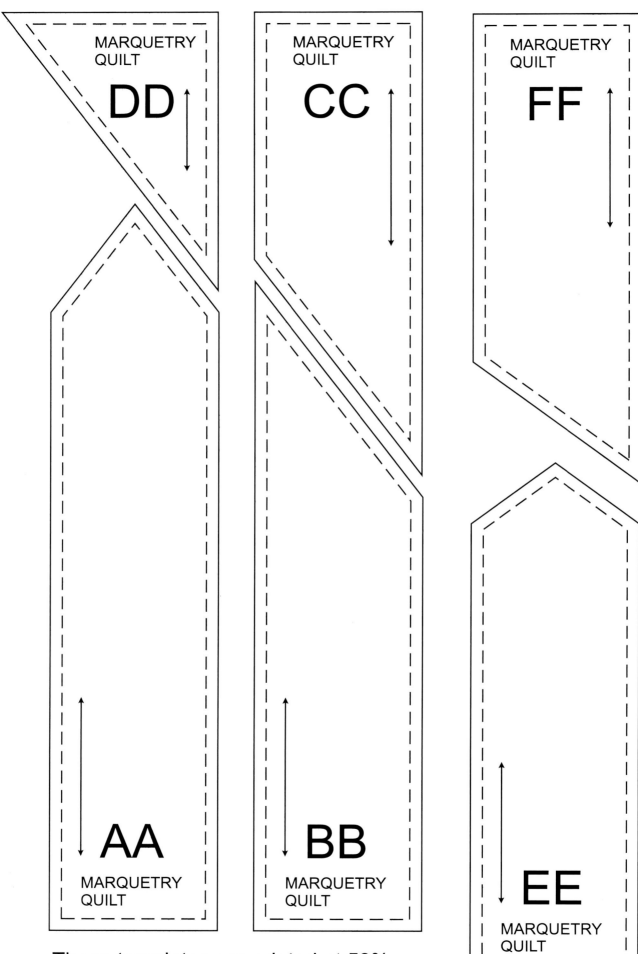

MARQUETRY
QUILT

DD

MARQUETRY
QUILT

CC

MARQUETRY
QUILT

FF

AA

MARQUETRY
QUILT

BB

MARQUETRY
QUILT

EE

MARQUETRY
QUILT

These templates are printed at 50% of real size. To use, scale them up 200% on a photocopier.

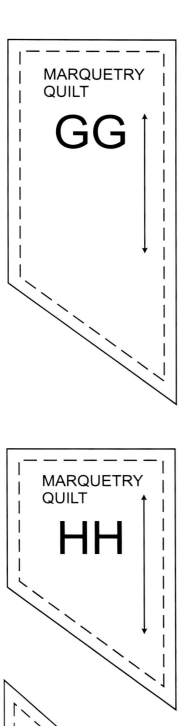

MARQUETRY
QUILT

GG

MARQUETRY
QUILT

HH

MARQUETRY
QUILT

II

MARQUETRY
QUILT

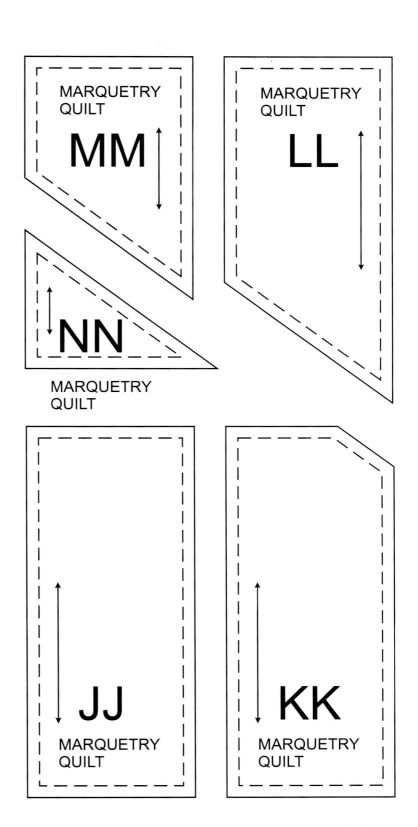

MARQUETRY
QUILT

MM

MARQUETRY
QUILT

LL

NN

MARQUETRY
QUILT

JJ

MARQUETRY
QUILT

KK

MARQUETRY
QUILT

These templates are printed at 50%
of real size. To use, scale them up
200% on a photocopier.

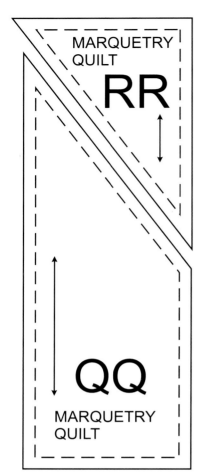

MARQUETRY QUILT

RR

QQ

MARQUETRY QUILT

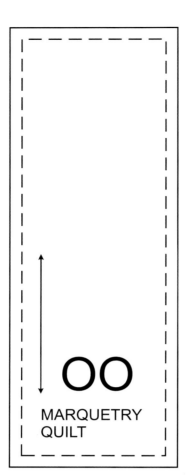

OO

MARQUETRY QUILT

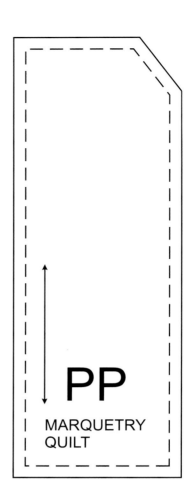

PP

MARQUETRY QUILT

These templates are printed at 50% of real size. To use, scale them up 200% on a photocopier.

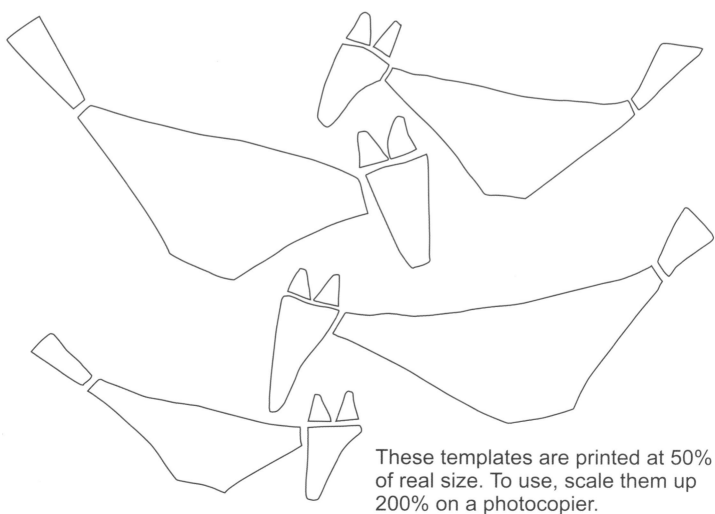

These templates are printed at 50% of real size. To use, scale them up 200% on a photocopier.

PATCHWORK KNOW-HOW

These instructions are intended for the novice quilt maker and do not cover all techniques used in making patchwork and patchwork quilts. They provide the basic information needed to make the projects in this book, along with some useful tips. Try not to become overwhelmed by technique - patchwork is a craft which should be enjoyed.

Preparing the fabric

Prewash all new fabrics before you begin, to ensure that there will be no uneven shrinkage and no bleeding of colours when the quilt is laundered. Press the fabric whilst it is still damp to return crispness to it.

Making templates

Templates are the best made from transparent template plastic, which is not only durable, but allows you to see the fabric and select certain motifs. You can also make them from thin stiff cardboard if template plastic is not available. If you choose cardboard, paint the edges of the finished template with nail polish to give it longer life.

Templates for machine-piecing

1 Trace off the actual-sized template provided either directly on to template plastic, or tracing paper, and then on to thin cardboard. Use a ruler to help you trace off the straight cutting line, dotted seam line and grainlines. Some of the templates in this book are so large that we have only been able to give you half of them. Before transferring them on to plastic or card, trace off the half template, place the fold edge up to the fold of a piece of paper, and carefully draw around the shape. Cut out the paper double thickness, and open out for the completed template.

2 Cut out the traced off template using a craft knife, ruler and a self-healing cutting mat (see page 101 for definition).

3 Punch holes in the corners of the template, at each point on the seam line, using a hole punch.

Templates for hand-piecing

• Make a template as shown above, but do not trace off the cutting line. Use the dotted seam line as the outer edge of the template.

• This template allows you to draw the seam lines directly on to the fabric. The seam allowances can then be cut by eye around the patch.

Cutting the fabric

On the individual instructions for each patchwork, you will find a summary of all the patch shapes used.
Always mark and cut out any border and binding strips first, followed by the largest patch shapes and finally the smallest ones, to make the most efficient use of your fabric. The border and binding strips are best cut using a rotary cutter.

Rotary cutting

Rotary cut strips are often cut across the fabric from selvedge to selvedge. With the projects we do, be certain to cut the strips running the desired direction.

1 Before beginning to cut, press out any folds or creases in the fabric. If you are cutting a large piece of fabric, you will need to fold it several times to fit the cutting mat. When there is only a single fold, place the fold facing you. If the fabric is too wide to be folded only once, fold it concertina-style until it fits your mat. A small rotary cutter with a sharp blade will cut up to 6 layers of fabric; a large cutter up to 8 layers.

2 To ensure that your cut strips are straight and even, the folds must be placed exactly parallel to the straight edges of the fabric and along a line on the cutting mat.

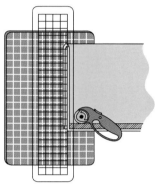

3 Place a plastic ruler over the raw edge of the fabric, overlapping it about ½in (1.25cm). Make sure that the ruler is at right angles to both the straight edges and the fold to ensure that you cut along the straight grain. Press down on the ruler and wheel the cutter away from yourself along the edge of the ruler.

4 Open out the fabric to check the edge. Don't worry if it's not perfectly straight; a little wiggle will not show when the quilt is stitched together. Re-fold fabric as shown in step 1, then place the ruler over the trimmed edge, aligning edge with the markings on the ruler that match the correct strip width. Cut strip along the edge of the ruler.

Using templates

The most efficient way to cut out templates is by first rotary cutting a strip of fabric the width stated for your template, and then marking off your templates along the strip, edge to edge at the required angle. This method leaves hardly any waste and gives a random effect to your patches.
A less efficient method is to fussy cut, where the templates are cut individually by placing them on particular motifs or stripes, to create special effects. Although this method is more wasteful it yields very interesting results.

1 Place the template face down on the wrong side of the fabric, with the grain line arrow following the straight grain of the fabric, if indicated. Be careful though - check with your individual instructions, as some instructions may ask you to cut patches on varying grains.

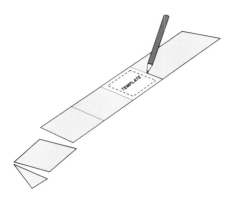

2 Hold the template firmly in place and draw around it with a sharp pencil or crayon, marking in the corner dots or seam lines. To save fabric, position patches close together or even touching. Don't worry if outlines positioned on the straight grain when drawn on striped fabrics do not always match the stripes when cut - this will add a degree of visual excitement to the patchwork!

3 Once you've drawn all the pieces needed, you are ready to cut the fabric, with either a rotary cutter and ruler, or a pair of sharp sewing scissors.

Basic hand- and machine-piecing

Patches can be joined together by hand or machine.

Machine stitching is quicker, but hand assembly allows you to carry your patches around with you and work on them in every spare moment. The choice is yours. For techniques that are new to you, practise on scrap pieces of fabric until you feel confident.

Machine-piecing

Follow the quilt instructions for the order in which to piece the individual patchwork blocks and then assemble the blocks together in rows.

1 Seam lines are not marked on the fabric, so stitch ¼in (6mm) seams using the machine needle plate, a ¼in- (6mm-) wide machine foot, or tape stuck to the machine as a guide. Pin two patches with right sides together, matching edges.

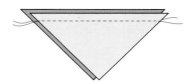

Set your machine at 10-12 stitches per inch (2.5cm) and stitch seams from edge to edge, removing pins as you feed the fabric through the machine.

2 Press the seams of each patchwork block to one side before attempting to join it to another block.

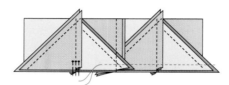

3 When joining rows of blocks, make sure that adjacent seam allowances are pressed in opposite directions to reduce bulk and make matching easier. Pin pieces together directly through the stitch line and to the right and left of the seam. Remove pins as you sew. Continue pressing seams to one side as you work.

Hand-piecing

1 Pin two patches with right sides together, so that the marked seam lines are facing outwards.

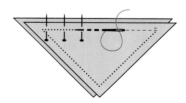

2 Using a single strand of strong thread, secure the corner of a seam line with a couple of back stitches.

3 Sew running stitches along the marked line, working 8-10 stitches per inch (2.5cm) and ending at the opposite seam line corner with a few back stitches. When hand piecing never stitch over the seam allowances.

4 Press the seams to one side, as shown in machine piecing (Step 2).

Inset seams

In some patchwork layouts a patch will have to be sewn into an angled corner formed by the joining of two other patches. Use the following method whether you are machine or hand-piecing. Don't be intimidated - this is not hard to do once you have learned a couple of techniques. The seam is sewn from the centre outwards in two halves to ensure that no tucks appear at the centre.

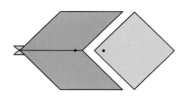

1 Mark with dots exactly where the inset will be joined and mark the seam lines on the wrong side of the fabric on the inset patch.

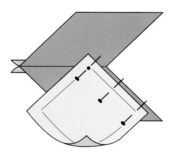

2 With right sides together and inset piece on top, pin through the dots to match the inset points. Pin the rest of the seam at right angles to the stitching line, along one edge of an adjoining patch.

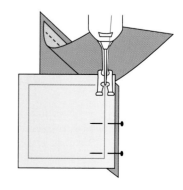

3 Stitch the patch in place along the seam line starting with the needle down through the inset point dots. Secure thread with a backstitch if hand-piecing, or stitch forward for a few stitches before backstitching, when machine-piecing.

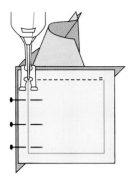

4 Pivot the patch, to enable it to align with the adjacent side of the angled corner, allowing you work on the second half of the seam. Starting with a pin at the inset point once again. Pin and stitch the second side in place, as before. Check seams and press carefully.

Curved seams

In some patchwork blocks such as Drunkard's Path a curve seam is pieced. Use the following method whether you are machine or hand piecing your blocks.

1 Cut your fabric pieces using the templates provided making sure to follow grain lines. Mark on any registration dots.

2 On the curved edges make 4-6 tiny snips with sharp scissors to help ease the fabrics together.

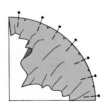

3 Place the pieces right sides together and pin at both ends. Ease the pieces until the edges match and pin in place. Sew using a ¼in (6mm) allowance.

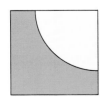

4 Open the block and press.

Foundation piecing

In foundation piecing, the patchwork design is worked onto paper patterns the exact size of each finished block, including seam allowances. During the stitching process, the patches are joined together by sewing through the foundation pattern to form the finished block.

Working Foundation – Umbrella Quilt

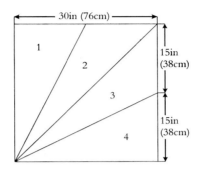

1 Take four 30in (76cm) square sheets of paper. Divide the papers into sections as shown in diagram 1 and number the sections on each paper, cut on the diagonal lines. These are your foundation papers. IMPORTANT: The papers will not have a seam allowance so make sure your fabric strips overlap the edges by at least ¼in (6mm).

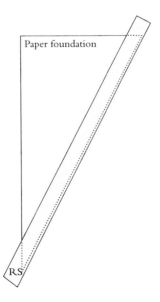

2 Place your first strip right side facing up, at a random angle on the edge of the first foundation paper (always have the numbers facing up) and pin into place.

3 Take the second strip and place right side down to match the first strip inside edge. Set your machine to a very

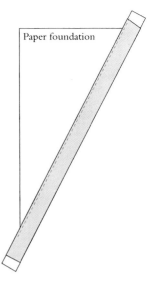

short stitch, this will make removing the papers much easier later. Stitch ¼in from the edge through all the layers.

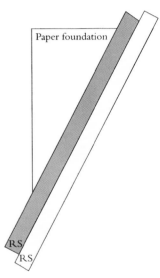

4 Fold the second strip back and press. See diagram 4. Add the next strip and continue in the same way until the whole paper is covered. Trim the edges leaving a ¼ in (6mm) allowance all around. Note: If you start to run short of any fabrics just piece off-cuts together into strips and use these in the same way as your cut strips.

5 Complete all the foundation papers in the same way varying the angles and orders of the stripes as you prefer. Do not remove the papers yet!

Machine appliqué

Using adhesive web:
To make machine appliqué even easier you can use adhesive web, which comes attached to a paper backing sheet, to bond the motifs to the background fabric. This keeps the pieces in place whilst they are being stitched.

1 Trace the appliqué design onto tracing paper. Reverse the tracing paper to reverse the image. Place the adhesive web (paper side up) over the reversed image and trace the motifs leaving a ¼in gap between all the shapes. Roughly cut out the motifs ⅛in outside your drawn line.

2 Bond the motifs to the back of your chosen fabrics. Cut out on the drawn line with very sharp scissors. Remove the backing paper by scoring in the centre of the motif carefully with a scissor point and peeling the paper away from the centre out, this prevents damage to the edges. Place the motifs onto the background noting any which may be layered. Cover with a clean cloth and bond with a hot iron (check instructions for temperature setting as adhesive web can vary depending on the manufacturer).

3 Using a contrasting or complimenting coloured thread in your machine, work small close zigzag stitches around the edge of the motifs making sure all the raw edges are stitched. Other decorative stitches can be used such as blanket stitch if you machine has them or you can stitch by hand.

Machine appliqué method for Hazy Sunshine Quilt:

1 Stitch the segments together to make fans and half fans. Stitch a basting line ¼in from the top and bottom edges of each fan. Clip the bottom edge (tightest curve) on each fan with sharp scissors 3 or 4 times just short of the basting line.

2 Turn the top and bottom seam allowances under on each fan following the basting line, Finger press. Pin the fans to each pieced background row in the sequence indicated in the layout diagram.

3 Stitch each fan into place very close to the top and bottom edges using a toning or decorative thread. Carefully remove the basting stitches. Press. You may if you wish cut the excess fabrics away from behind the fans to remove bulk.

Hand appliqué

Good preparation is essential for speedy and accurate hand appliqué. The finger-pressing method is suitable for needle-turning application, used for simple

shapes like leaves. Using a card template is the best method for bold simple motifs such as circles.

Finger-pressing:

1 To make your template, transfer the appliqué design on to stiff card using carbon paper, and cut out template. Trace around the outline of your appliquéd shape on to the right side of your fabric using a well sharpened pencil. Cut out shapes, adding a ¼ in (6mm) seam allowance all around by eye.

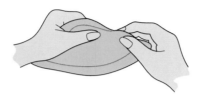

2 Hold shape right side up and fold under the seam, turning along your drawn line, pinch to form a crease. Dampening the fabric makes this very easy. When using shapes with 'points' such as leaves turn the seam allowance at the 'point' in first as shown in the diagram, then continue all round the shape. If your shapes have sharp curves you can snip the seam allowance to ease the curve. Take care not to stretch the appliqué shapes as you work.

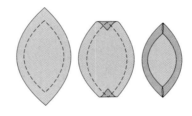

Card templates:

1 Cut out appliqué shapes as shown in step 1 of finger-pressing. Make a circular template from thin cardboard, without seam allowances. You will need a separate template for each circle.

2 Using a matching thread, work a row of running stitches close to the edge of the fabric circle. Place thin cardboard

template in the centre of the fabric circle on the wrong side of the fabric.

3 Carefully pull up the running stitches to gather up the edge of the fabric circle around the cardboard template. Press, so that no puckers or tucks appear on the right side. Then, carefully pop out the cardboard template without distorting the fabric shape.

Pressing stems

For straight stems, place fabric strip face down and simply press over the ¼ in (6mm) seam turning along each edge.

Needle-turning application:

1 Lay stems on to the right side of your block and tack in position down centre of stem.

2 Pin on the first leaf, right side up, tucking one end under the tacked stem. Starting close to the stem, stroke the seam allowance under with the tip of the needle as far as the creased pencil line, and hold securely in place with your thumb. Using a matching thread, bring the needle up from the back of the block into the edge of the leaf and proceed to blind-hem in place (see below). Work around the whole shape, stoking under each small section before sewing. Appliqué additional leaves in the same manner, and then the stalk in place.

3 Pin and tack flower heads to top of stems, then appliqué the flowers in place with blind-hemming stitch and a matching thread.

Blind-hem stitch

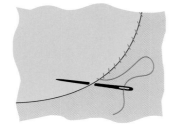

This is a stitch where the motifs appear to be held on invisibly. Bring the thread out from below through the folded edge of the motif, never on the top. The stitches must be worked small, even and close together to prevent the seam allowance from unfolding and frayed edges appearing. Try to avoid pulling the stitches too tight, as this will cause the motifs to pucker up.

Mitreing Borders.

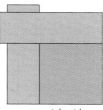

right side

1 Centre the borders along the sides of the quilt and then stitch each into place stopping ¼ in (6mm) from the end of the quilt centre.

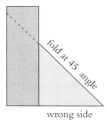

fold at 45 angle

wrong side

2 Working on each corner in turn, fold the quilt at a 45 degree angle and stitch from the intersection of the two border seams to the outer edge of the borders as shown in the diagram. The stitching line should in effect extend the folded edge of the quilt.

right side

3 Open out the quilt and check the borders lay flat and the angle is correct. Finally, trim the excess border fabric back to ¼ in.

Quilting and finishing

When you have finished piecing your patchwork and added any borders, press it carefully. It is now ready to be quilted and finished.

Preparing the backing and batting

*   Remove the selvedges and piece together the backing fabric to form a backing at least 3in (7.5cm) larger all round than the patchwork top. There is no need to allow quite so much around the edges when working on a smaller project, such as a baby quilt.

*   For quilting choose a fairly thin batting, preferably pure cotton, to give your quilt a flat appearance. If your batting has been rolled up, unroll it and let it rest before cutting it to the same size as the backing.

Basting the layers together

1 On a bare floor or large work surface, lay out the backing with wrong side uppermost. Use weights along the edges to keep it taut.

2 Lay the batting on the backing and smooth it out gently. Next lay the patchwork top, right side up, on top of the batting and smooth gently until there are no wrinkles. Pin at the corners and at the midpoints of each side, close to the edges.

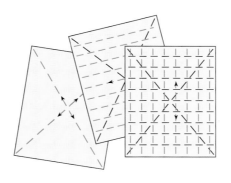

3 Beginning at the centre, baste diagonal lines outwards to the corners, making your stitches about 3in (7.5cm) long. Then, again starting at the centre, baste horizontal and vertical lines out to the edges. Continue basting until you have basted a grid of lines about 4in (10cm) apart over the entire quilt.

4 For speed, when machine quilting, some quilters prefer to baste their quilt sandwich layers together using rust-proof safety pins, spaced at 4in (10cm) intervals over the entire quilt.

Transferring quilting designs and motifs

The tool you use to mark your quilting design on to the fabric must be carefully chosen. Because of the variables of fabric in both colour, texture and fabric surface, no one marker can be recommended. It would be a terrible shame to have made your patchwork quilt up to this stage and then spoil it with bad marking! It is therefore advisable to test out various ways of marking on scrap pieces of fabric, to test how clearly you can see the marks, and whether any lines that show after stitching can be sponged or washed away.

Chalk-based markers: these include dressmakers' chalk pencils, and powdered chalk markers. These are available in a variety of colours, and leave a clear line which often disappears during stitching or is easily removed by a brush. Chalk pencils must be kept sharpened to avoid making thick lines.

Pencils: silver and soapstone pencils available from specialist shops, both produce clear lines, which are almost invisible after quilting. Coloured pencils can be used on darker fabrics, and water-erasable ones mean the lines can be sponged away after stitching.
Pale fabrics present difficulties for marking with pencils. If you choose a lead pencil, make sure it's an 'H' type, which will leave only a fine thin line.

Perforating: the design can be transferred from a paper template on to fabric by running a tracing wheel over the outlines. With many fabrics the dotted line will last long enough for work or a portion of it to be completed.

Dressmakers' carbon paper: The carbon paper is placed working side down, between the paper template and fabric. The design can then be drawn on by tracing around the design with a pencil, or running over the design with a tracing wheel to produce a dotted line. It is available in a number of colours, for both light and dark fabrics.

Quilters' tape: a narrow re-usable sticky-backed tape, which can be placed on to the fabric surface, to provide a firm guideline for quilting straight-line patterns and grids.

Quilting through paper: some fabrics are difficult to mark for machine quilting. In these instances the design can be transferred on to tracing paper, which can be pinned to the surface of the quilt. The quilting is then done by stitching through the paper, which is then carefully torn away after quilting with the help of a blunt seam ripper.

Templates: some designs require templates, especially if a design is repeated. These can be used as an aid to help draw patterns either directly on to the quilt surface, or when drafting a design full-sized on to paper. With outline templates only the outside of the design can be drawn - any inner details will need to be filled in by hand.

Stencil templates can be made at home, by transferring the designs on to template plastic, or stiff cardboard. The design is then cut away in the form of long dashes, to act as guides for both internal and external lines. These templates are a quick method for producing an identical set of repeated designs.

Hand quilting

This is best done with the quilt mounted on a quilting frame or hoop, but as long as you have basted the quilt well, a frame is not necessary.

With the quilt top facing upwards, begin at the centre of the quilt and make even running stitches following the design. It is more important to make even stitches on both sides of the quilt than to make small ones.

Start and finish your stitching with back stitches and bury the ends of your threads in the batting.

Machine quilting

- For a flat looking quilt, always use a walking foot on your machine for straight lines, and a darning foot for free-motion quilting.

- It's best to start your quilting at the centre of the quilt and work out towards the borders, doing the straight quilting lines first (stitch-in-the-ditch) followed by the free-motion quilting.

- When free motion quilting stitch in a loose meandering style as shown in the diagrams. Do not stitch too closely as this will make the quilt feel stiff when finished. If you wish you can include floral themes or follow shapes on the printed fabrics for added interest.

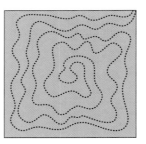

- Make it easier for yourself by handling the quilt properly. Roll up the excess quilt neatly to fit under your sewing machine arm, and use a table, or chair to help support the weight of the quilt that hangs down the other side.

Preparing to bind the edges

Once you have quilted or tied your quilt sandwich together, remove all the basting stitches. Then, baste around the outer edge of the quilt ¼in (6mm) from the edge of the top patchwork layer. Trim the back and batting to the edge of the patchwork and straighten the edge of the patchwork if necessary.

Making the binding

1 Cut bias or straight grain strips the width required for your binding, making sure the grainline is running the correct way on your straight grain strips. Cut enough strips until you have the required length to go around the edge of your quilt.

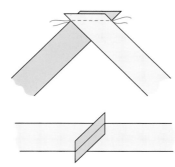

2 To join strips together, the two ends that are to be joined must be cut at a 45 degree angle, as above. Stitch right sides together, trim turnings and press seam open.

Binding the edges

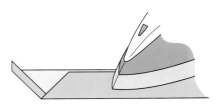

1 Cut starting end of binding strip at a 45-degree angle, fold a ¼in (6mm) turning to wrong side along cut edge and press in place. With wrong sides together, fold strip in half lengthways, keeping raw edges level, and press.

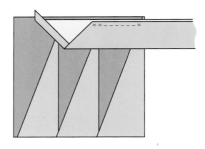

2 Starting at the centre of one of the long edges, place the doubled binding on to the right side of the quilt keeping raw edges level. Stitch the binding in place starting ¼in (6mm) in from the diagonal folded edge (see above). Reverse stitch to secure, and working ¼in (6mm) in from edge of the quilt towards first corner of quilt. Stop ¼in (6mm) in from corner and work a few reverse stitches.

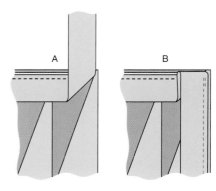

3 Fold the loose end of the binding up, making a 45-degree angle (see A). Keeping the diagonal fold in place, fold the binding back down, aligning the raw edges with the next side of the quilt. Starting at the point where the last stitch ended, stitch down the next side (see B).

4 Continue to stitch the binding in place around all the quilt edges in this way, tucking the finishing end of the

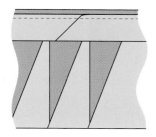

binding inside the diagonal starting section (see above).

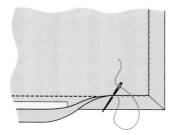

5 Turn the folded edge of the binding on to the back of the quilt. Hand stitch the folded edge in place just covering binding machine stitches, and folding a mitre at each corner.

Completing the Cushions

Note: Use a ⅜in (1cm) seam allowance throughout and stitch seams with right sides together, unless otherwise stated.

1 Press a double ½in (1.2cm) hem to the wrong side of 1 long edge on both large and small cushion backs, and stitch in place close to first pressed edge.

2 Place the larger back, face down, on to the right side of the cushion front with raw edge level and the hemmed edge set back from one of the front edges. Place the smaller back, face down, on top of the uncovered side of the front cushion, keeping raw edges level and overlapping the hemmed edges.

3 Baste the cushion cover pieces together. Turn cover through to right side and insert cushion pad through centre back opening.

How to prepare a Quilt or Patchwork for hanging

To keep your patchwork flat when hanging on a wall, insert wooden dowels through channels at the top and base of the hanging. To do this, cut 2 strips of fabric 1¾in wide (4.5cm) x the width of your quilt. Press raw edges of each strip ⅜in (1cm) to the wrong side, and then slipstitch the strips to the wrong side of the hanging at the top and base, along the long pressed edges. Insert ⅜in- (1cm-) diameter wooden dowels cut 5cm shorter than width of quilt and slipstitch ends of channels closed.
To hang the wall hanging, stitch a brass ring to each end of top channel and use to hook them over picture hooks, or nails.

GLOSSARY OF TERMS

Appliqué The technique of stitching fabric shapes on to a background to create a design. It can be applied either by hand or machine with a decorative embroidery stitch, such as buttonhole, or satin stitch.

Backing The bottom layer of a *quilt sandwich*. It is made of fabric pieced to the size of the quilt top with the addition of about 3in (7.5cm) all around to allow for quilting take-up.

Basting Also known as tacking in Great Britain. This is a means of holding two fabric layers or the layers of a *quilt sandwich* together temporarily with large hand stitches, or pins.

Batting Also known as wadding in Great Britain. Batting is the middle layer, or *padding* in a quilt. It can be made of cotton, wool, silk or synthetic fibres.

Bias The diagonal *grain* of a fabric. This is the direction which has the most give or stretch, making it ideal for bindings, especially on curved edges.

Binding A narrow strip of fabric used to finish off the edges of quilts or projects; it can be cut on the straight *grain* of a fabric or on the *bias*.

Block A single design unit that when stitched together with other blocks creates the quilt top. It is most often a square, hexagon, or rectangle, but it can be any shape. It can be pieced or plain.

Border A frame of fabric stitched to the outer edges of the quilt top. Borders can be narrow or wide, pieced or plain. As well as making the quilt larger, they unify the overall design and draw attention to the central area.

Butted corners A corner finished by stitching *border* strips together at right angles to each other.

Chalk pencils Available in various colours, they are used for marking lines, or spots on fabric. Some pencils have a small brush attached, although marks are easily removed.

Cutting mat Designed for use with a *rotary cutter*, it is made from a special 'self-healing' material that keeps your cutting blade sharp. Cutting mats come in various sizes and are usually marked with a grid to help you line up the edges of fabric and cut out larger pieces.

Darning foot A specialist sewing machine foot that is used in *free-motion* quilting – the *feed dogs* are disengaged so that stitches can be worked in varying lengths and directions over the fabric.

Ditch quilting Also known as *quilting-in-the-ditch* or *stitch-in-the-ditch*. The quilting stitches are worked along the actual seam lines, to give a *pieced quilt* texture. This is a particularly good technique for beginners as the stitches cannot be seen - only their effect.

Dressmakers' carbon paper Also known as tracing paper. Available in a number of colours, for light or dark fabric. It can be used with pencils, or a tracing wheel to transfer a quilting design on to fabric.

Feed dogs The part of a sewing machine located within the *needle plate* which rhythmically moves up and down to help move the fabric along while sewing.

Foundation pattern A printed base exact size of a *block* onto which patchwork pieces are sewn. The foundations are usually made from soft paper, but could also be lightweight fabric, interfacing, or one of the new non-woven tear-away backings, such as *Stitch-n-tear*.

Free-motion quilting Curved wavy quilting lines stitched in a random manner. Stitching diagrams are often given for you to follow as a loose guide.

Fussy cutting This is when a template is placed on a particular motif, or stripe, to obtain interesting effects. This method is not as efficient as strip cutting, but yields very interesting results.

Grain The direction in which the threads run in a woven fabric. In a vertical direction it is called the lengthwise grain, which has very little stretch. The horizontal direction, or crosswise grain is slightly stretchy, but diagonally the fabric has a lot of stretch. This grain is called the *bias*. Wherever possible the grain of a fabric should run in the same direction on a quilt *block* and *borders*.

Inset seams, setting-in or Y-seams A patchwork technique whereby one patch (or block) is stitched into a 'V' shape formed by the joining of two other patches (or blocks).

Iron-on interfacing eg. Vilene/Pellon. A non-woven supporting material with adhesive that melts when ironed, making the interfacing adhere to the fabric.

Mitred Binding A corner finished by folding and stitching binding strips at a 45-degree angle.

Mitred Borders Borders where the corners are joined at a 45-degree angle.

Needle plate The metal plate on a sewing machine, through which the needle passes via a hole to the lower part of the machine. They are often marked with lines at $\frac{1}{4}$in (5mm) intervals, to use as stitching guides.

Padding Also known as *batting* in the United states and *wadding* in Great Britain, this is the middle layer of a *quilt sandwich*. Padding can be made of cotton, wool, silk or synthetic fibres and can be bought in sheets or as a loose stuffing.

Paper-backed adhesive web eg. Bondaweb/Wonder-Under. Can be cut to shape and pressed to the wrong side of a fabric shape using a hot iron. Then the paper backing is peeled off. The fabric shape can then be placed on top of another, adhesive side down, and pressed again to fuse in place.

Patch A small shaped piece of fabric used in the making of a *patchwork* pattern.

Patchwork The technique of stitching small pieces of fabric (*patches*) together to create a larger piece of fabric, usually forming a design.

Pieced quilt A quilt composed of *patches*.

Pins Use good quality pins. Do not use thick, burred or rusted pins which will leave holes or marks. Long pins with glass or plastic heads are easier to use when pinning through thick fabrics. Safety pins (size 2) can be used to 'pin-baste' the quilt layers together.

Quilters' tape A narrow removable masking tape. If placed lightly on fabric, it provides a firm guideline for straight-line patterns.

Quilting Traditionally done by hand with running stitches, but for speed modern quilts are often stitched by machine. The stitches are sewn through the top, *padding* and *backing* to hold the three layers together. Quilting stitches are usually worked in some form of design, but they can be random.

Quilting foot See *walking foot*.

Quilting frame A free-standing wooden frame in which the quilt layers are fixed for the entire quilting process. Provides the most even surface for quilting.

Quilting hoop Consists of two wooden circular or oval rings with a screw adjuster on the outer ring. It stabilises the quilt layers, helping to create an even tension.

Quilt sandwich Three layers of fabric: a decorative top, a middle lining or *padding* and a *backing*. Collectively known as the 'quilt sandwich'. They are held together with quilting stitches or ties.

Rotary cutter A sharp circular blade attached to a handle for quick, accurate cutting. It is a device that can be used to cut up to six layers of fabric at one time. It needs to be used in conjunction with a 'self-healing' *cutting mat* and a thick plastic ruler.

Rotary ruler A thick, clear plastic ruler printed with lines that are exactly $\frac{1}{4}$in (6mm) apart. Sometimes they also have diagonal lines printed on, indicating 45 and 60-degree angles. A rotary ruler is used as a guide when cutting out fabric pieces using a *rotary cutter*.

Sashing A piece or pieced sections of fabric interspaced between blocks.

Sashing Posts When blocks have sashing between them the corner squares are known as sashing posts.

Selvedges Also known as *selvages*, these are the firmly woven edges down each side of a fabric length. Selvedges should be trimmed off before cutting out your fabric, as they are more liable to shrink when the fabric is washed. They are also difficult to quilt due to the firm nature of the weave.

Setting-in See *Inset seams*.

Stitch-in-the-ditch See *ditch quilting*.

Stitch-n-tear A new non-woven material resembling a non-woven interfacing which is used underneath fabric to support it while embroidering, or patchworking by machine. When the stitching is completed the material is simply torn away.

Staystitches Rows of directional machine stitches, placed just inside certain seamlines, to prevent them from stretching out of shape during handling and construction. The most important seamlines to staystitch are those that are curved or angled. Staystitching is done immediately before or after removing your pattern, and is worked through a single layer of fabric.

Tea-dyeing The use of tea for dyeing fabrics gives a subtle aged look to new fabric. Many methods can be used but there are two simple methods. For darkening and ageing specific areas of a quilt dab the area with a wet tea bag until the tea has darkened the area to your preferred level. Let the area dry, this will set the tea stain. Use very mild soap when the quilt is washed or the dyeing will fade. For a large quilt when you want an all over effect, steep 20 tea-bags in a litre of boiling water for 20 minutes. Remove the tea-bags and pour the liquid into a dye-bath. Add warm water and mix, then add the quilt. Let the quilt sit in the tea until it has taken the level of dye you prefer. Then remove and wash the quilt in very mild soap. It should be noted that the fabrics may be affected by the tannic acid in tea and may deteriorate earlier than normal.

Template A pattern piece used as a guide for marking and cutting out fabric *patches*, or marking a *quilting*, or *appliqué* design. Usually made from plastic or strong card that can be reused many times.

Threads One hundred percent cotton or cotton-covered polyester is best for hand and machine piecing. Choose a colour that matches your fabric. When sewing different colours and patterns together, choose a medium to light neutral colour, such as grey or ecru. For both hand and machine *quilting* it helps to use coated or pre-waxed quilting thread, which allows the thread to glide through the quilt layers. Hand quilting can be worked in special threads, such as pearl or crochet cotton.

Tracing wheel A tool consisting of a spiked wheel attached to a handle. Used to transfer a design from paper on to fabric, by running the wheel over design lines.

Tying A quick and easy way to hold the *quilt sandwich* layers together without using machine or hand *quilting*. Thread or yarn is inserted through the quilt layers at regular intervals and tied in a knot or bow, or secured with a stitch or buttons.

Unit A small part of a patchwork design made from *patches*, which is then pieced together with other units to form a *block*.

Wadding The British term for *batting*, or *padding* (inner filling).

Walking foot Also known as a *quilting foot*, this is a sewing machine foot with dual feed control. It is very helpful when quilting, as the fabric layers are fed evenly from the top and below, reducing the risk of slippage and puckering.

Y-seams See *inset seams*.

KAFFE FASSETT FABRICS USAGE LIST

See pages 25 – 29 for full range of fabric swatches. See the list below for fabric and page number.

Alternate Stripe
AS01: 39
AS03: 44, 46
AS10: 44

Artichokes
GP07-C: 70
GP07-J: 34
GP07-L: 34
GP07-S: 34, 42
GP07-P: 54, 66, 78

Blue and White Stripe
BWS01: 42
BWS02: 42, 70

Broad Check
BC01: 57, 72
BC02: 57
BC03: 57
BC04: 57

Broad Stripe
BS01: 40, 46, 62
BS08: 46
BS11: 46

Exotic Check
EC01: 57
EC02: 57
EC03: 57
EC05: 57

Chard
GP09-J: 72
GP09-C 54
GP09-P 78

Damask
GP02-C: 54, 78
GP02-J: 34, 72
GP02-L: 78
GP02-P: 34, 42, 54, 78
GP02-CT: 72, 78
GP02-S: 42, 54, 78

Exotic Stripe
ES21: 39

Forget Me Not Rose
GP08-C: 48, 72, 78
GP08-L: 72, 78
GP08-S: 42, 54, 72, 78

Gazania
GP03-C: 72
GP03-P: 72
GP03-S: 42

Narrow Check
NC01: 57

NC02: 57
NC03: 57, 72
NC05: 57

Narrow Stripe
NS01: 40, 44, 46
NS17: 62, 72

Ombre Stripe
OS02: 42
OS05: 42

Pachrangi Stripe
PS01: 46
PS05: 44
PS15: 57

Pressed Roses
PR01: 42, 54
PR02: 40, 54
PR03: 70
PR04: 40
PR05: 40
PR06: 40
PR07: 70

Roman Glass
GP01-G: 34, 40, 50, 72
GP01-L: 34, 52, 72
GP01-P: 52, 72, 78
GP01-R: 34, 40, 72
GP01-PK: 72
GP01-BW: 40, 68, 70
GP01-S: 34, 50
GP01-C: 40, 72

Rowan Stripe
RS01: 50, 60, 72
RS02: 48, 72
RS03: 40
RS04: 34, 50
RS05: 40, 64, 66, 72
RS06: 66
RS07: 34, 50, 66, 68, 72
RS08: 54

Shot Cotton
SC01: 44, 57, 64
SC02: 57, 81
SC04: 57, 62, 64
SC05: 57, 62, 64, 68, 70
SC06: 57
SC07: 44, 46, 57, 62, 81
SC08: 44, 57, 62, 64
SC09: 44, 62, 81
SC10: 44, 57, 62, 81
SC11: 39, 57, 60, 62, 81
SC12: 39, 57, 72
SC13: 46, 57
SC14: 37, 38, 39, 57, 62, 64, 66, 72

SC15: 57
SC16: 39, 57, 62
SC17: 34, 39, 57, 64, 66, 75
SC18: 57, 64, 50
SC19: 34, 39, 57, 62, 66, 72, 75
SC20: 57, 62
SC21: 46, 57, 75
SC22: 57, 66, 75
SC23: 57, 64, 75
SC24: 39, 42, 54, 57, 62, 72, 75
SC25: 75
SC26: 39, 42, 46, 66, 72, 75
SC27: 57, 72, 75
SC28: 70
SC29: 34, 37, 38, 42, 54
SC30: 60, 75
SC31: 34, 39, 64
SC32: 60, 72
SC33: 40, 48, 52, 60, 62, 68, 72, 81
SC34: 52, 60, 72
SC35: 40, 60, 62, 72
SC36: 37, 38, 40, 42, 66, 72
SC37: 37, 38
SC39: 37, 38, 48, 75
SC40: 48, 52, 75
SC41: 52, 68
SC43: 52, 72

Floral Dance
GP12-MG: 34, 72
GP12-O: 34, 72
GP12-MV: 34, 42
GP12-B: 34
GP12-P: 34, 72

Chrysanthemum
GP13-O: 34, 72
GP13-GN: 34, 72
GP13-B: 34
GP13-R: 34, 72
GP13-GR: 78

Dotty
GP14-C: 34, 52
GP14-P: 34, 52, 72
GP14-O: 34, 50, 72
GP14-T: 34, 78
GP14-D: 34, 42, 50, 66, 72, 78
GP14-L: 34, 66, 72, 78
GP14-SG: 34, 66, 72, 78

Bubbles
GP15-O: 34, 50, 72
GP15-G: 34, 42, 50, 66, 72
GP15-P: 34, 52
GP15-C: 34, 52
GP15S: 34, 72

INDEX

<table>
<tr><td colspan="2">

ABBREVIATIONS

The Kaffe Fassett Fabric collection

Stripes

NS	Narrow stripe
PS	Pachrangi stripe
ES	Exotic stripe
AS	Alternate stripe
BS	Broad stripe

FQ   a 22½in x 20in (57cm x 50cm) piece of fabric, sold as a 'fat quarter'.

W.S wrong side.

</td></tr>
</table>

Experience ratings

★   Easy, straightforward, suitable for a beginner.

★★ Suitable for the average patchworker and quilter.

★★★ For the more experienced patchworker and quilter.